Memories

of

Basingstoke

The publishers would like to thank the following companies for their

support in the production of this book

Main Sponsor
W Webber Limited

RW Armstrong & Sons Limited

The Automobile Association

Basingstoke College of Technology

Berry Bros & Rudd

Fyffes

Oxoid Limited

Rawlings Transport

Wella

Winterthur Life

First published in Great Britain by True North Books Limited
England HX5 9AE
Telephone: 01422 377977
Copyright © True North Books Limited, 2000

ISBN 1 903204 26 7

Text, design and origination by True North Books Limited
Printed and bound by The Amadeus Press Limited

Introduction

U p until the 1960s, Basingstoke was a small market town in north Hampshire. The name has a Saxon origin and the town had a weekly market before 1086.The development of this market town over the centuries was gradual and 'natural'. By the 1960s its main streets were full of small shops with a couple of larger stores. Major employers were Wallis & Stevens (traction engines etc), Thornycrofts (particularly well known for the Mighty Antar tank transporter, Queen Mary low loaders and bren gun carriers) and the clothing manufacturers Burberry's, Mares and Gerrish Ames & Simpkins. All showed clear roots in Basingstoke's agricultural interests: agricultural machinery, the wool trade, brewing and malting.

The shape of the town was compact. The River Loddon flowing from the west (starting in fact at West Ham) gave its name to the east-west Brook Street. From there Wote Street and Church Street came up the hill to join Winchester Street and London Street. Other roads that radiated out to places near or far from Basingstoke and showed what destinations were important to the town, were Reading Road, Sarum Hill (the Salisbury Road), Aldermaston Road, Kingsclere Road, Hackwood Road and Cliddesden Road.

But what a change was to come! It was decided to enlarge the town around this nucleus as an overspill for the excess population of London. With the influx of people came housing estates, a new shopping area, and commercial and industrial estates, bringing many new employers. The railway was electrified and the M3 motorway gave another link to London.

This had been a small town, where everyone knew or recognised most people. Now some of the loveliest houses were pulled down. Demolition reduced large areas to waste land before new buildings arose on a quite different scale. To many people Basingstoke now seems a new town with new housing estates all round - oddly enough, as they were built, it was discovered that these sites had been occupied before by little farmsteads of the Iron Age and Roman period, about a mile apart from one another.

Now the town began to fill up with people from what seemed almost another world - Londoners! The following pictures and captions show the town through the 1930s to the late 1960s. For those who don't know what the old town looked like, this book will give you just a glimpse of its streets and people.

Contents

A right royal occasion

<big>R</big>eports of the celebrations held to mark George V's Coronation in 1937 mention services held in St Michael's, the Church Street Methodist church and the Roman Catholic church of the Holy Ghost. Other churches in the town were the Congregational church in London Street, the Baptist church in Sarum Hill and the Immanuel Chapel of the Countess of Huntingdon's Connexion in Wote Street. The picture shows Webber's on the left, a draper's shop. The Crown Restaurant next door took its name from an old inn that was round the corner in Winchester Street. This inn had another entrance where the restaurant is in the picture. On the opposite side, the hoarding hides the building of some new shops and borough offices that take the place of shops burnt down in 1935.

Winchester Street, straight ahead, is seen here with decorations for the 1935 Jubilee celebrations for King George V. The shop on the right is Lansley's. It was pulled down in 1962 to build a more modern shop. Victoria Street, coming in from the right, was built after 1902 and once was the site of the first bus depot. On the other corner is the Golden Gate restaurant, serving its customers throughout the 1930s. There were few cars at this time, so women could gossip on the corners without fear of getting run over! No central lines on the road meant that cars didn't always stay on their right side.

Above (both pictures): The 1935 parade down London Street, in honour of George V's Silver Jubilee. George V came to the throne in 1910 and reached his Silver Jubilee in 1935. Basingstoke always seemed to take any chance to celebrate, especially with parades through the town. These pictures show just a small part of the procession. A list appears in the programme for the day and included the order of the procession. In one picture we have the fire brigade marching along, following B Company of the 4th Battalion Hampshire Regiment. The firemen were followed by the police in their smart uniforms, and then the town's magistrates. In the background you can see Boots the Chemist, which opened in 1925 in part of the old Bell Inn. The Bell had once housed a debtors' prison. The Marquis of Winchester, who led the Civil War defence of Basing House in the years 1642 to 1645, was imprisoned in the Bell Inn after the House fell. Oliver Cromwell stayed in the Fleur de Lys Inn opposite and from here he sent a letter to Parliament about his victory. A plaque to commemorate this was unveiled in October, 2000. The Marquis was sent to London for trial but was eventually released and returned to Hampshire.

Wote Street was earlier called Oat Street or Ote Street. In 1865 a corn exchange opened at the top of the street. Later it became a cinema, called the Grand, then a roller skating rink and now it is the Haymarket Theatre. On the far right of the picture is the shop of George Willis. He was the founder of the town museum, a watchmaker and for many years on the town council, becoming alderman and then mayor. He was the first person to be made a 'Freeman of Basingstoke' in recognition of all that he had done for the town. His old shop still serves the community but is now called The Sandwich Shop. A replica of Willis's shop is being erected in the new Milestones Museum. Opposite the theatre is the Feathers Hotel. This is a very old inn. There is a will of 1640 containing an inventory of the premises. Each of the bedrooms is named and one is called 'the Swan'. It had two bedsteads, valued at £6.10s. The garden at the rear was sometimes used as a theatre. Samuel Attwood recorded in his diary of 1824, 'Mr Bridge opened a temporary theatre called 'The Pavilion' in the Feathers Inn garden.' Wote Street once led to the Basingstoke canal basin. The canal brought business to the town's shops and pubs but was never very profitable. Many stretches of the canal are still open and used for pleasure boating but it no longer comes into Basingstoke. After it closed, the canal basin became White's Timber Yard and later still it became the bus station.

Left: These Red Cross nurses are walking through the Market Place and passing the Town Hall, which in the 1980s became the Willis Museum. The programme says that the Salvation Army should be next but it's the St John's Ambulance Brigade. Perhaps it's more logical that they followed the nurses. These people all had their part to play in the war that started a few years later. There were lots of events that people could go to, to celebrate the Jubilee, such as motor cycle sports, gymnastics and boxing. There was a fly-past by heavy bombers from RAF Worthy Down. Free meals were provided for children and old age pensioners. The day ended with a bonfire and a firework display. The local newspaper adds some interesting facts to the occasion. The Gazette tells us that only one baby was born on that day. She was born to Mr & Mrs Whatley of 84 George Street. We wonder if she still lives in the area. Burberry's put on a mannequin display in their store. Tea and cigarettes were provided and a wireless set was used to entertain the watchers with music. Many people ended the day by going out into the country to see a series of beacons being lit. Two of the highest were on Farleigh Hill and Beacon Hill.

Above: Brook Street and Lower Brook Street, running east to west, followed the line of an old trackway out of town, leading to West Ham and Worting. Part of it used to be called Frog Lane and 'Brook' refers to the River Loddon. Brook Street had large houses like Brook House, which became the High School for Girls (now in Crossborough Hill and known as Harriet Costello). May's Brewery and a farm took up a large area. Then came 'Noah's Island', so named because it was surrounded by branches of the river Loddon. It is now the site of the Victory Roundabout. Then, to the west, Lower Brook Street was often, as in this photograph, also referred to as 'Brook Street'. It provided Victorian terraced housing for the workers who came to the town in the 19th century to work for the railways, breweries and engineering firms. We can see that the street is still lit by gas lamps and the bicycle reigns supreme over the motor car. What had once been a market town was developing into an industrial town. Now it is full of offices and computer organisations. The picture shows decorations for the Jubilee celebrations of King George V that took place on 6 May 1935. This happened on a Monday and the children in the photograph have the day off. They are not wagging school! Apart from watching a procession through the town, the people in Brook Street could attend entertainments put on by the Entertainments Committee and the children could join in organised games. There was also a tea laid on for women and children and a dinner provided for old age pensioners. The day ended with a bonfire and fireworks. This part of Lower Brook Street was demolished in 1968 as part of the new town development.

Left: Some buildings have many lives! This picture shows one of the town's four cinemas, the Plaza, which started life as a drill hall for K Company of the 1st Hants Rifle Volunteers in 1885. It was built for Lt Col John May, six times mayor of Basingstoke. Over the years it hosted royal celebrations, banquets and dances. Later, when it became the Plaza cinema, it showed films with stars of yesteryear, such as Nelson Eddy, Jeanette MacDonald and Gracie Fields. The film showing in the picture arrived in Basingstoke in 1935 and the bunting celebrates the Jubilee of King George V. To celebrate the 1937 coronation of George VI, all four cinemas gave free showings for 1,900 local children. The Plaza alone gave away 670 tickets. The children had to go to the place mentioned on their tickets. The Plaza closed down in 1954 and the building ended its life as a furniture store for the Portsea Island Co-operative Society. The Plaza was at the top of Sarum Hill, the old Salisbury road. At the bottom of Sarum Hill, a tank trap was put in front of Henry Thornton's shop and bakery during the second world war and removed quite soon after, but six more between the houses on the left, as you go down the hill, stayed there till 1983.

Below: Winchester Street was the place to come for the larger shops of the town. On the left is Lanham's. This large store was a draper's, and a ladies' and gents' outfitters. They were also footfitters and shoe repairers, house furnishers and undertakers. At the back, their yard extended round the corner into New Street, where their other shop sold china, glassware and ironmongery. Lanham's took over the premises from Thomas Burberry in 1914. Burberry's was one of the major employers in the town, famous for the gabardine raincoats worn by kings and prime ministers. This waterproof material went to the South Pole with Shackleton and Scott. Also Roald Amundsen, the first man to reach the South Pole, wore Burberry overalls on his epic trip. In October 2000 Thomas Burberry's great-grand-daughter unveiled a plaque outside Burberry's former showroom. Opposite Lanham's is Marks and Spencer, which was built in 1934 on the site of an earlier doctor's house and a separate surgery.

The street is seen here decorated beautifully for the 1935 Jubilee celebrations.

This is half way up Church Street, looking towards the Market Square. The clock tower on the Town Hall had been there since 1887, when they were celebrating Queen Victoria's Golden Jubilee. The tower was dismantled in 1961 but a part of the clock remains, a few feet lower than it used to be, on the second floor of the museum. The date of the photograph is late 1930s, so the flags and bunting probably celebrate the Coronation of George VI in 1937. The shop on the left nearest the camera is Norris & Neate, high-class ladies' hairdressers. Terry Hunt, who took some of the photos in this book, at one time had premises next door. On the opposite side is The Warren, previously George Stevens, a newsagent's. Mr Milward is said to have made his first pair of shoes on these premises - the birth of the chain of Milward's shoe shops to be found in many towns. Recent eerie goings on above this shop had the workers thinking the place was haunted.

Both pictures: It was a warm welcome that the Duke of Gloucester received on arriving in Basingstoke on his first visit of his one-day Boy's Club Tour in July 1938. He was in the first car, a Humber, one of only three of this marque built for the royal family. Three other Humbers carried VIPs, with a police escort. They had come into town via Worting Road and Essex Road, which were lined with cheering crowds. Here he is in Brook Street, not far from his destination, the Toc H Boys' Club. The Duke, who had been staying with Lord Portal at Laverstoke House, reached the town at about 10.30 am, where the Mayoress, Mrs Edith Weston was immediately presented to him. Here he is *(bottom picture)* outside the entrance of the Toc H Boys' Club. This was over the offices and showrooms of the Basingstoke Timber Company (housed in the silk mill which had been used by the Salvation Army which came to the town to preach against the evils of drink in 1882). He is wearing a double-breasted suit, whereas most of the other men have single-breasted jackets. Does the umbrella suggest rain? In July?! Notice the old camera on the right. Who was this man snapping for? The woman to his left is Miss Mary 'Betty' Davis, who was a wonderful alto in the Basingstoke Operatic Society

and All Saints choir. The Duke made a lightning tour of the club, visiting each room to watch the boys' activities. He saw the boys' committee room, the carpenter's shop, the library, the lecture room, the large games room and the canteen. Having completed his tour of the premises, the Duke departed from the town, cheered on by a crowd of well-wishers. He could not have stayed long, as he was in Odiham by eleven o'clock! He left town via Brook Street, Church Street and London Street. After Odiham, he went on to Winchester and finally arrived at Thorney Island aerodrome, where his plane took him back to London. His tour of the clubs took about nine hours altogether.

The Town hall is decorated for the Coronation of Queen Elizabeth in 1953. The Town Hall stopped being the council offices in 1921 but stayed open for dances and other activities until it became the Willis Museum.

Our Royalty has made a number of visits to Basingstoke: Henry III came in 1226 and Henry VII in 1499. Catharine of Aragon stayed with Mr Kingsmill in London Street on her way to meet her betrothed, Henry VIII, and Philip and Mary passed through to spend their honeymoon at Basing House after their wedding in Winchester Cathedral. Queen Elizabeth I stayed at Basing House and visited the Holy Ghost Chapel in 1592, while Queen Elizabeth II opened the AA building in 1973. Prince Charles opened the town's Sports Centre in 1970 and visited Lansing Bagnall's factory in 1979. The late Diana Princess of Wales visited Church Cottage in 1986, arriving in a swirl of leaves as she stepped down from a helicopter in the War Memorial Park.

Both pictures: The Queen opens the AA headquarters in 1973. Here the Queen is in the shopping centre before opening the tall AA building on the Basing View business estate. The building, known by millions as Fanum House, was completed on time for a mere £4,412,000. It has eighteen floors and rises to 220 feet. From the viewing gallery at the top you get a very good view of the town and the countryside round about. Although the town keeps growing, the countryside is still within easy distance for most inhabitants.

The Queen planted a tree at the entrance and unveiled an inscription in the entrance hall to commemorate the occasion. Percy Sainsbury, the Council's 'Jack of all trades', had two jobs on this day, he put out the barriers that you see in the picture and straightened some of the lampposts with a crane. The mayor, Councillor Alan Turner, accompanies the Queen. Wherever the Queen goes, you will find policemen and photographers. Here you can see both.

At leisure

The bandstand in the Memorial Park used to be a popular place to go on Sunday afternoons. This park was originally the parkland of an 18th century house called Goldings which became the Town Clerk's office and is now the Register office. The bandstand was originally erected in another park, near Fairfield School, about 1901 and in 1921 it was moved to its present site. There used to be iron seats around the bandstand.

The music, played by the town's Silver Band and by Silver Bands from Tadley or Hannington, was rather different from that being played in the dance halls. Now bands play in Eastrop Park. Eastrop Park incorporates the River Loddon, which flows through a paddling pool and two lakes before leaving at the other end of the park. The water features make this park very popular, especially in the summer.

It's the late 50s and Father Christmas has arrived at Curry's to receive requests. His toy bill must have been a lot smaller in those days with prices like those in the picture - £4.19s 6d! Lots of things were sold in those days for something and sixpence. Today it's something and 99p. Shopkeepers are still trying to tell you it's less than you think! Curry's in London Street was a small branch of a national chain of electrical shops. It first opened in 1927 in Church Street, moved to London Street in 1935, to the new shopping centre in 1971 and out to the Brighton Hill retail site in 1996. We wonder if the children got their wishes! If any of you three are reading this book, can you remember? Old money disappeared in February 1971, although you can still find some coins in our museums.

Below: The Mimets were a local pop group, entertaining at a local hall in the sixties. The town had a number of well-known disc jockeys. Johnny Prince was one of them, he later became a town councillor. Chubb Dyer and Jim Miller were two others. At weekly dances held in the town hall and other venues, pop groups that went on to become famous would bop the night away. A bit of name-dropping includes Lulu and the Luvvers, Georgie Fame, Little Eva, Wayne Fontana, The Troggs, The Who, the Nashville Teens, the Yardbirds, David Bowie, The Tornados, The Ivy League, Screaming Lord Sutch and his Raving Savages, The Animals, The Moody Blues, The Hollies, The Small Faces, the Kenny Everett Show and Stevie Wonder. Lesser-known groups had such names as The Wooley Bears, The Habits, Falling Leaves, The Evil Eyes, The Hoochie Coochie, The T Bones and The Fingers!

Bottom: Children on the way home from school, crossing Brook Street. St John's School was built in 1901 because St Michael's Church had so many children attending Sunday school every week. It soon became a day school for 130 boys and girls plus 230 infants. It was built on the site of a farmhouse owned by Mr Portsmouth, whose farm was in Eastrop. You can visit his family tomb at Eastrop's St Mary's church. Before that it was a hospital built by Walter de Merton for elderly clergymen. Walter founded Merton College, Oxford and many of these clergy had been scholars there.

An elephant on a rainy day outside the railway station! We know that it can be boring waiting to buy your ticket and standing on draughty platforms but would British Rail really hire an elephant to entertain would-be passengers?! No, it was part of a visiting circus, one of several that came to Basingstoke in the 1950s. The animals were unloaded from a special train and led through the streets to a large tent. When Mr Tomlin, an estate agent from Wote Street, returned from a three-month tour of South Africa, he was surprised to find elephants outside the Railway Station. He hadn't seen any in Africa! Percy Sainsbury worked for the local council. One day his foreman sent him to a house where a huge hole had appeared in someone's garden. The tree that had been there the day before had disappeared down the hole. There was a rumour that one of the circus elephants had died. Was this where it had been buried? When Percy investigated, he did not find any elephant bones but a rotten board that had been covering a soakaway and had collapsed, taking the tree and grass down with it! Some of the other stories that Percy tells included removing a dead dog, a dead deer and a boy stuck firmly in some mud. The most bizarre tale was when a double-decker bus tried to go under a railway bridge. It lost its upper deck, so came out a single decker!

Street scenes

Above: Although it's not much of a square in shape, Winton Square was popular with the horses because it had a horse trough. However, one of the local buses took a dislike to the trough and tried to remove it. Someone did remove the trough some time in the 1950s. The Square got its name from Winton House, which had at one time been a girls' boarding school. The bookshop on the left of the picture, called Durants, ran a library for members. It also sold books, magazines, sweets and all types of stationery. During the second world war it became the local food office for the Ministry of Food, where you queued for your ration books. Recently the sign for the food office was discovered and safely removed. Next to it is a greengrocer, Wilkinson's, then Mayfair, a sweets and tobacco shop run by Miss Dykes. Scards motor and cycle depot was there for many years, providing parts, petrol and oil. After that was Coombes, a ladies' outfitter's. The church at the end is the Primitive Methodist church, erected in 1902 at a cost of £4,643. It was pulled down in 1970 after the Trinity Methodist church was built just down Sarum Hill, on the right of the picture. Opposite, not seen in the photo, was the Wheatsheaf Hotel. It was a coaching inn in the 18th century and its yard was also used when farmers and others came in to hire workers at Michaelmas, when a fair and stalls were set up in the streets.

Upper Wote Street, with a good view of the Town Hall clock tower. On the right is the Haymarket Theatre. Basingstoke has been a market town for most of its life and corn and cattle dominated the area. You bought and sold your corn from factors who worked from the lower ground floor of the Town Hall. In 1865 they opened a corn exchange, now the Haymarket, and business flourished. You could also buy and sell animals in the large hall of the exchange. They even held dinners there on occasion. The fire engine was kept in the basement and horses had to be brought from the Railway Arms when there was a fire. More recently, the basement housed the offices of the St John's Ambulance Brigade as well as public conveniences. General Booth, the founder of the Salvation Army, held a service in the exchange in the 1880s. In 1910 Mr Watkins of Alton bought the building and opened a roller skating rink. Occasionally boxing took place inside. In 1913 the use changed to a cinema, with seats, a projector room and special lighting. It started with silent films and then they bravely brought in the 'talkies' - could these really catch on? The building was gutted by fire in 1925 and re-opened later. In 1940 the Council renovated the building and soon Basingstoke had its own professional acting company. As the Haymarket Theatre, it is still a popular venue today, where many TV stars have appeared in plays and musicals. It was Dr Radford Potter who thought up the name Haymarket, Hay for corn and market for exchange. A bit corny you might think.

Above: A snowy market day during the winter of 1962. This picture shows some hardy stall-holders serving some even hardier shoppers. Only two stalls were set up, because of the weather. An earlier snowstorm in April 1908 was so severe that it brought down a great number of telephone poles, cutting off the phones of 1,000 subscribers. The Town Tall clock became clogged with snow and stopped at about one o'clock and the St Michael's church clock stopped at twenty past two. The Market Square has seen scenes like this for hundreds of years. The town had a market in 1086 AD when the Domesday Book was compiled for William the Conqueror. Did it use the same area that it uses today? We will never know. When the present Town Hall was erected in 1832, the Market Square was also changed. In 1851 the local farmers boycotted the market because the town council imposed tolls and for a time they held their market outside the Bolton Arms in Old Basing until the council gave in.

Lloyds Bank can be seen behind the two market stalls. In 1806 a Mr Raggett, with other partners, set up a bank on the other side of the road. The Hampshire Banking Company bought this and in 1888 it changed its name to the Capital and Counties Bank. This is where Lloyd's comes in. They bought out the Capital and Counties Bank in 1918, and in 1927 Lloyd's built the imposing building that you see in the background of this picture. Arthur Attwood describes bags of money being pushed across the road on a trolley from the old premises.

Susan Richmond started work in Lloyd's Bank in the 1940s at the age of 15. Her supervisor was Mary Felgate. Susan remembers her time at the bank. 'Can you believe it? We had to wear a coat and hat in those days at the bank. I worked on the accountant machine - well, it was a computer really. It was a National Cash machine and ran on electricity. It was a great typewriter with a small typewriter down at the bottom ... and you put in these ledger pages. There were eight huge ledgers and there were four of us with two ledgers each. The working hours were 8.45 until everything had balanced! On a slack day like Thursday, which was half day closing, you could be out by four o'clock - if everything balanced. You could spend hours looking for a penny. You didn't get paid overtime. My first salary was £1 a week with a shilling deducted for sick benefit, (the Manchester Unity of Oddfellows). So I got 19 shillings. Just twice a year, on 30 June and 31 December, we did get a shilling if we worked past seven. Someone would run out and get some cakes or buns or sandwiches, or something like that. That was when we did the bank charges, that all had to be put through on one day. On 31 December we were lucky if we got to a New Year's Eve Party! But we did get New Year's Day off - that was a Bank Holiday.'

This is a fine example of the problem of parking that the town experienced in the 1950s. All the buildings went in the 1960s, to be replaced by a high wall that formed the rear of the new shopping centre. This land had once been a hospital for retired clergy, then a farmhouse owned by Mr Portsmouth, and then St John's School. The River Loddon ran along the bottom of Church Street and there was at one time a wooden bridge, the remains of which were discovered when building was going on. The area used to be prone to flooding in the wet weather, and even today, in heavy rain, water still streams down Church Street, Wote Street and New Street.

Two shops on the left of this photo of Winchester Street are Milward's and Chesterfield's. Alfred Milward started a boot and shoe business in his living-room in Church Street. He had a hawker's licence and he used a horse and cart to call on the gentry in an effort to build up his business. In 1957, a hundred years after he started his business, there were Milward shops in 39 towns in the south of England. Reading had the first branch. In an advert in the 1918 programme for the celebrations at the end of

the first world war, Milward's claimed to have the largest and most up-to-date ladies and children's footwear in this district. 'Our Gents' Department is now replete with footwear of the highest grade.' In August 1996 it was taken over by Clarke's. In contrast, the shop next door was Chesterfield's, the outfitter's. It was established in 1913 and only recently, in 1995, did it close. It was one of the last of the old shops of the town and it was sad to see its passing. Further along there used to be a popular billiard hall above Burton's.

The policeman on duty is helping traffic come out of Wote Street, in front of him. Edna Fielding says, 'I remember cycling up here and the policeman put his hand up, so I had to stop. My front wheel was just over the white line, so he made me get off and walk back behind the line, 'Go on! Back! Back!' In July 1960 a one-way system was introduced which allowed traffic to head west along Southern Road and east through the town centre. The first traffic warden to risk his life in Basingstoke told a driver, 'You can't park here'. He was met with derision. In the old days you could park anywhere in the Market Place. Now you have to get a permit and if you stay a minute over time, well! All these roads were open to traffic in the 50s. Now they are pedestrianised and it's only skateboards and the occasional delivery vehicle that might mow you down. The two main streets that join the Market Place are London Street, going towards London, and Winchester Street, leading to the older capital of England. In the 1950s you would have been able to shop at Woolworth's, Curry's and Boots along these two roads. Ada Wilson, who ran the Opera Restaurant in the late fifties, had to fight the Council to be able to put up her sign. She needed it because the café was upstairs. When it opened, lunches were 3s 6d with meals such as 'bacon roly poly and vegetables'. Later the menu was more extensive and expensive. Some of the first 'lunchers' were farm boys on market days, later office workers, doctors and shopkeepers. She also did birthday parties for children. In later years the restaurant had a juke box. The International Store was one of a chain of stores nation-wide. Someone who worked in the store described what she had to do. 'People gave their order to the assistant behind the counter, who looked out each item for you. We had to know all the stock in our section, the different spices etc. There was a compulsory seat at the end of the counter but one manager didn't allow the assistants to sit on it. In a bitter winter he wouldn't have the doors closed and there was no heating in the shop. It wasn't easy to serve with chilblains on your fingers.' For six weeks before Christmas the assistants had to 'work on', weighing everything up and packing it for the special orders for the 'Christmas Club'. Sometimes the assistants didn't get home till half past twelve at night. But they enjoyed it, singing carols and popular songs of the day as they worked and not a penny overtime! By 1958 the International Store was a self-service store.

Left: Lanham's in Winchester Street replaced Burberry's nine years after the Burberry Emporium was burnt down in 1905. Thomas Burberry began his world famous organisation in Winchester Street in the 1850s. Ruby Philpott said of Lanham's , 'It was a lovely shop. At Christmas they had the most beautiful bazaar in the basement, with a fairy and a Father Christmas. I remember one Christmas they had someone dressed in a bearskin and it frightened me to death.' Apprentices at Lanham's started at the grand wage of 2/6d a week, plus commission. But they didn't get very much commission because above them was the junior and above the junior would be the buyer and of course they served before the apprentices. But there was the chance of promotion at the end of the three-year apprenticeship. The apprentices had to do all the odd jobs that nobody else would do. Many of the staff actually lived over the shop at this time.

Above: A traffic jam in Winchester Street. This is a familiar sight in Basingstoke, even today with traffic lights everywhere and roundabouts. It was an Easter Monday in the late 1950s. The Race Meeting had just ended at Hackwood Park, outside Basingstoke. The traffic spilling out onto the A30 held up London-bound holidaymakers, returning from the coast. Motorists trying to avoid the snarl-up on the Basingstoke Bypass tried in vain to find a quicker route through the town itself. Giffords, on the corner, was a cycle shop. This form of transport would have been a quicker way to get to where they were going. Lord Montagu of Beaulieu was once caught speeding in a speed trap in Winchester Street (not on the day this picture was taken, but in 1900 - it's not the present Lord Montagu!) The summons, issued on 15 April by Superintendent Thomas Hale, stated that on Good Friday Lord Montagu was travelling at 21 miles per hour when the speed limit was only 12 miles per hour. He was fined £1 with 12d costs! It didn't help to be rich and famous.

This view of Basingstoke, taken from the top of the Town Hall in 1960, shows Church Street, with St Michael's church dominating the centre. Top right are the Holy Ghost ruins, often seen from trains that pass through Basingstoke's station. The large white building on the far left is Eli Lilly's, the pharmaceutical company. The factory was built in 1939, just before the second world war. Its white exterior made it a target for any stray bomber coming this way, so it had to be camouflaged. Eli Lilly's was founded in America

in 1876 and in 1999 the firm celebrated the 60th anniversary of its arrival in Basingstoke. As you look at all these rooftops, you notice chimney stacks with round chimney pots on top. It won't be long before people forget what those strange objects were and that they were used to clear smoke from the rooms below, where people lit fires in a fireplace. Will they remember a rumour that it was down these chimneys that Santa Claus used to come with presents for children and eat hundreds of mince pies and drink a glass of wine or sherry?

Below: A 'three-wheeler' is parked in the street. You don't see many of them now. People are crossing the road without having to wait for heavy traffic to clear. Many of the shops here moved downhill to the new shopping centre in the 1960s. The Halifax Building Society had the tall building next to the outfitters, Chesterfield's. At the time of writing it is now empty, awaiting a new tenant or owner. The building further down with columns was Burton's and James Walker. Many of the facades of these shops have changed over the years, but the top storeys have remained much as they were in the 19th and 20th centuries. The second shop on the left was a watch maker in the 19th century called Gregory's and an old picture shows it decorated for the Golden Jubilee of Queen Victoria in 1887. The shop was established in 1790.

Right: A go-slow in Winchester Street in the 1960s. The hotel on the right is the Victoria Hotel, closed in 1970. The building became a discothéque for some years. The building on the left became the Co-op and when it was pulled down the Museum Archeological Group did a rescue dig and found mediaeval and post-mediaeval pottery in pits.

London Street was made a one-way street in 1960. Most of the small shops in this part of town are now gone. Greig's on the left still serves rolls, sandwiches, hot pies and great bread pudding! Woolworth's started here in 1921 and moved down the hill to the new shopping centre in 1970. Opposite is a gent's outfitter called Butler's, established in 1925, where you can buy good quality men's wear and be kitted out for a wedding. However, you can't catch a bus, because in 1976 the street was pedestrianised. The bus stop in the picture was the outside the Congregational Church, now the United Reform Church. London Street was for a very long time one of the main thorough-fares for the town. Fifty coaches would travel along this stretch most days during the coaching boom of the 18th and early 19th centuries. In the 17th century Oliver Cromwell slept in one of its inns and wrote a letter to Parliament about his Civil War victory at Basing House.

Bottom: When the Town Hall, which is on the right of this stall, was opened in 1832, the ground floor was an open space that earlier stallholders could hire. They had a roof over their heads but no walls to stop wind and rain. This space was enclosed in 1865 and rooms were provided for the Town Clerk and the magistrates to change into their robes and for reading.

Right: Church Street now starts at the Market Place and runs down to Cross Street. On the left there used to be at least four inns and the entrance to another, the Crown, which was in Winchester Street. The four were the Ship, now part of Lloyds Bank, The Black Boy, which changed its name to the Hop Leaf for obvious reasons, the Eagle and further down was the Harrow. Another inn was the Self-Defence on the opposite side, in earlier years said to be frequented by local gypsies. Next to this inn was the St John's primary school, opened in 1901. Inns were multipurpose establishments. They were meeting places for friends, for clubs and for food, drink and a bed for the night. When the railway came in 1839, the stage-coaching days of the town were numbered and so were many of the inns.

The picture shows one of the town's problems: parking. Once you could park in the streets but now there are various car parks and you have to pay.

Memorable moments

This parade took place just after a new mayor was sworn in. The Salvation Army Band is leading the procession down Church Street. When the 'Sally Army' first came to Basingstoke in the 1880s they marched against the 'demon drink'. Well, the town did have about 80 drinking houses for a population of about 4,000. The local drinking population versus the local church-going population greatly upset the peace of the town. As the Salvation Army marched, they were surrounded by mobs shouting in praise of drink. The real army had to be called out and the Riot Act read from the steps of the Town Hall. Some of the ringleaders were put on trial at Winchester and when they returned they were welcomed back with a banquet!

Most of the buildings on the left are now gone or greatly altered. Southwell's was a bakery. The town hall clock tower went in 1961. The cast iron support was beginning to crack and was in danger of falling through the roof. As with most of the pictures in this book, the men you see are mostly wearing suits and ties. Not a sight you would see nowadays in our streets.

Below right: There was a weekly market for farm animals on a Wednesday, run by the Raynbird family. The main market was up by the railway station. Mr Dorkins, 'Dorky' to most people, would ring a bell to call the farmers out of the nearby Station Hotel bar, informing them that the next cattle sale was about to take place. Some of the animals made it back to a farm somewhere to be milked or for breeding. If they were underweight they also had to return to their farms to chew more cud! Local butchers would drive the sheep, cows and pigs down Station Hill and down Wote Street or Church Street to their own slaughterhouse. Some turned into the gap near the Feathers Hotel. Basingstoke Cattle Market handled over 4,000 cattle in 1950. Horse sales were held on the first Wednesday of each month. Donkeys and ponies were also sold. Even the Royal Family ate Basingstoke meat. In 1947 two bullocks, three calves, ten sheep and five pigs joined the Royal Yacht on its trip to South Africa. The Philpott bakers in Potter's Lane once had a visit from two large pigs that got lost on the way to their fate. The door to the shop opened and noises were heard coming from the green-houses at the back and there were the two pigs. Were they

in hiding? The picture was taken early in 1960s By 1966 the cattle market had closed to make way for the new town development scheme. It had been there for over 90 years.

Bottom: The Hants Regimental Band marching down London Street on the day that they were given the 'Freedom of the Borough' in July 1966. The mayor who made the presentation was Councillor Harold Redstall. Brooks was a greengrocer's and fruiterer's, sandwiched between two chemists, Timothy White's and Boots, both of which later moved to the new shopping centre.

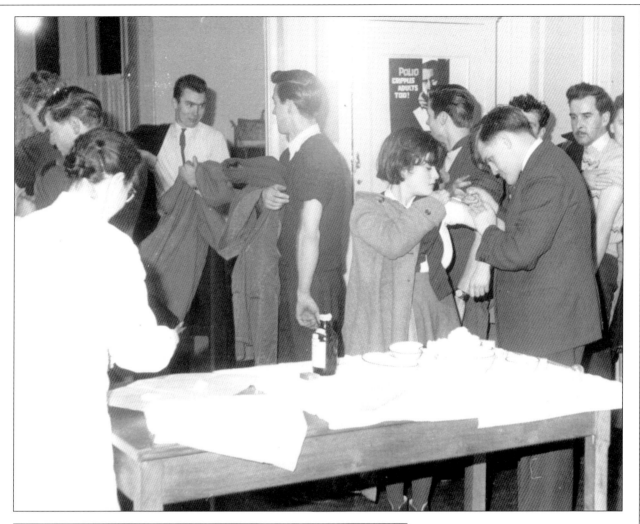

Above: A 1950s wedding group. You could say this is a dying practice in our modern era but some people still dress up, make vows, have a breakfast in the afternoon, make speeches and throw confetti. St Michael's has been the main place for weddings for centuries, and still is, though many weddings now take place in the Register Office at Goldings.

It is believed that the bride may have been a Carnival Queen for Basingstoke at one time.

Top: Smallpox scare! Dr Tom Roberts, who died in July 2000, was the medical officer for health in Basingstoke. Here he is giving people of all ages, not just children, an injection against smallpox in 1962. The epidemic had broken out in the Midlands and was thought that it might spread to all parts of our islands. The building is Brambly's Grange Health Centre, just off Winchester Road. Brambly's Grange had once been the house of Mr Thornycroft, Managing Director of Thornycrofts, the internationally known builder of ships at Woolston and and all kinds of vehicles at Basingstoke, including military vehicles, steam vans and the chassis for double-decker buses. Thornycrofts was one of the main employers in the town and helped to make the town prosperous. On their 50th anniversary in 1948, the workers had a day's holiday with pay and 250 guests were invited to a luncheon.

The Rectory garden party. Churches like to have their annual fetes and garden parties. This one was in the grounds of St Michael's Rectory in Church Street and took place some time in the late 1950s.

Apart from the cake stalls, hoop-la, ice cream, teas and the Bring and Buy stalls, there were other entertainments. One year a man stuck nails into himself. He didn't prove too successful an attraction, as many people turned away.

Now, what about the little boy near the camera? He's not posing for his picture. Is he looking for his mum or playing at running away and 'Come and get me', which is a favourite game with some small children? The house is no longer the rectory. A new one was built close by and the house, now called Chute House, is used by local clubs and charities. The garden at the back is now a small park (Glebe Gardens) with a quiet stream gently flowing through it.

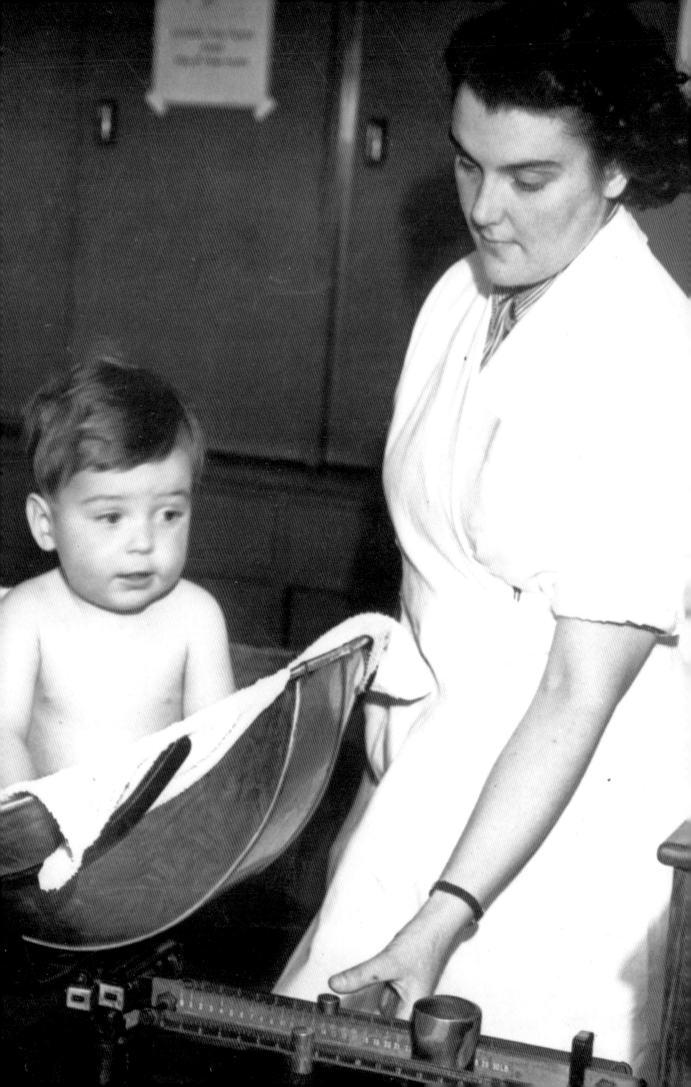

Both pages: It was possibly the acute wartime shortages of food and supplies which made doctors, health workers and mothers alike very aware of the health of the new generation, and children were carefully weighed, measured and immunised against the illnesses that had at one time meant disfigurement or even death *(facing page)*. A vaccine for polio, the scourge of former years which left behind its terrible mark of wasted and useless limbs, only came later, however. American scientist Jonas Edward Salk developed a vaccine in 1955, and an oral vaccine was produced in 1960. The vaccine brought the dreaded disease under control and today polio is rarely seen. On a day to day basis, vitamins were vital to the health of children, and long before the advent of the cod liver oil capsule, the recommended spoonful of cod liver oil was administered to the youngest children every day in schools and nurseries around the country during the 1940s. Children might have screwed up their noses at the fishy taste, but the nourishing cod liver oil went a long way towards keeping them healthy. The vitamin-packed orange juice was far more palatable, and artful mothers would often use the orange juice as a bribe: no cod liver oil, no orange juice. Following hard on the heels of the oil, the juice took away the distinctive taste that was disliked by so many children. Ante-natal clinics did all they could to check on the diet, blood pressure and vitamin intake of mothers to be; our carefully posed photograph, taken in an ante-natal clinic in the 1930s, records at least the cleanliness and tidiness that was to their great credit *(bottom)*. And when the tiny new citizen finally arrived, there were health visitors to pay friendly calls on families in their homes to check on the health and happiness of mothers and babies *(left)*. National Dried Milk for babies was also made available to mothers, and before today's push towards natural feeding NDM was for decades very much in vogue. We need to remember that at the time of these photographs the National Health service did not exist, and in fact the NHS only came into operation after World War II in July 1948.

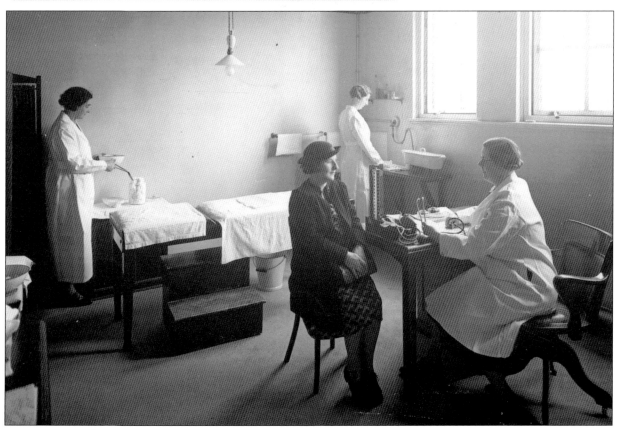

Bottom: This is the Tadley Wolf Pack assembled in the Market Place in Basingstoke. They were there to celebrate Jack Welling becoming the new mayor in 1955. Councillor Welling was chairman of the carnival committee for many years, arranging carnivals from 1956 onwards.

In 1955 the 26th Basingstoke group started with four scouters, 20 wolf cubs and 15 boy scouts. Meetings were held in the old community centre but later they moved to the Den, as wolves are more used to dens than they are to community centres! The 26th became the Tadley Scout Group in 1966.

Right: In the year that some English footballers won a small cup or something (mainly because of three brilliant players from West Ham United), these boys were on parade. They were part of the mayor's procession for 1966. They look serious so we expect they still have to endure the long walk through the town centre. If it were afterwards it would show on their faces! The mayor that year was Councillor Harold Redstall.

Wartime

Both pictures: This DUKW or terrapin *(left)*, an amphibious vehicle, is seen outside Thornycrofts where the prototypes were made. Arthur Attwood helped to make them from scratch. They had to be delivered to the Ministry within six weeks and after they had passed their sea trials they were sent to the Morris Cowley works for mass production. They were used in the D-Day landings. The bren gun carrier *(top)*, also made at Thornycrofts, is out on road trials in May 1940, near the Dorchester Arms on the A30. They used to go into the King George V playing field, where a water splash had been built for them.

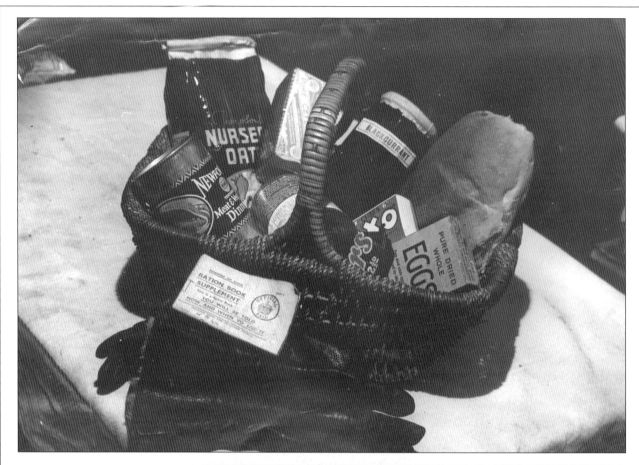

During the Second World War, the air raid sirens sounded over Basingstoke a total of 312 times. On a number of occasions, bombs and destruction followed. Following these raids, the local paper printed the following information: 12 people were killed, 21 seriously and 50 slightly injured, 25 properties were completely destroyed, 25 more were beyond repair and 856 suffered slight damage. This did not include places where the windows blew in under the force of the blast. The Basingstoke Museum, then in New Street, lost all its windows and did not open again for three years. It was estimated that all this damage was inflicted by only 26 bombs and one machine gun attack.

On 16 August 1940, German bombers were seen coming from the south. One of the leading planes dropped bombs on Church Street, Church Square and Church Lane. A second bomber dropped its load onto Burgess Road. A number of pictures were taken of Church Square after the bombing. Buildings were destroyed, windows were shattered and people were killed and injured. Victor Price, an evacuee, heard the bombers coming over on 16 August 1940. He was about ten years old and was standing in the doorway of his lodgings with his landlady, who was holding her baby. He described the next things he saw and did. 'It was a sunny day. Suddenly I saw this aircraft. Before I knew it, the bombs started falling out of it, and it wasn't very high up. So I shouted to Mrs Overton, "Get to the stairs!" and we all ran to the stairs. I shut the front door, but within seconds the bombs exploded. The front door blew open, and we just wondered what had happened.' He ran off to find out. He ran along Mortimer Lane and ended up in Church Square. 'The whole of the square looked devastated.' However, for a ten-year-old boy the square became a playground for

the next few years, for evacuees and town boys alike. He said, 'At the beginning there were quite a few houses there, which created a tremendous amount of excitement, going through cellars, looking for lumps of shrapnel from the bombs. This was the start of the war, as we knew it.' Arthur Attwood was a member of the Home Guard. He had been up all night at Thornycrofts, doing a 12-hour shift and at about five o'clock on Friday 16 August he was fast asleep. His wife, who was expecting their first child, heard the planes as the bombs fell. She reached the bedroom just as there was a mighty crash, which rocked the house.

Arthur describes what happened next. 'I did not need to be awakened. Instinctively, I raced downstairs and into the street, to see a great pall of dust and smoke over the town centre. As a member of the Home Guard, I dressed and hurried to see if any help was needed. I only got as far as the crossroads at the bottom of Church Street, which was sealed off by the military to allow the voluntary services to work without interruption. I returned home to wait and wonder, for one could only find out what happened by hearsay.' During that night an unexploded bomb in Church Square went off, destroying a Georgian house.

here is something wrong here, isn't there? 'NO RIGHT TURN.' If you were approaching this sign, which way would the right be? Would it be on the left or really on the right?! When Hackwood Road, Southern Road, Victoria Street, Winchester Street and London Street were made one-way in 1960, this sign was erected on its post still in its cardboard casing. Only when they tore off the covering did they realise their mistake. However, this did not happened until the 'great day' had arrived for all traffic to find alternative routes to their destinations. Then they took off the covering and with much haste the sign was reversed. Perhaps they could have sent it to Australia! The sign was at the junction where New Road and London Street met. In 1976 London Street, Winchester Street, Wote Street and Church Street were pedestrianised.

sandbags he couldn't and his sergeant had to rescue him before it went off.

Top: The Home Guard started life as the Local Defence Volunteers. They had uniforms but few rifles at first. Some had wooden rifles made so that they could drill with the rest of the Guard. Some of the men are not wearing hats. Is it a sign of shortage or of men with a rebellious streak? Much of the training took place after the men had been working a 12-hour shift. The picture shows men from the Thornycrofts Home Guard,

Above: You might think that children would want to watch soldiers marching past but these children seem more interested in something else. Thornycrofts lies behind the hedge that the soldiers are marching past. Mr Diffy, who kept this hedge so tidy, used to organise demonstrations of depth-charge throwers. The Home Guard volunteers were all shapes and sizes, and all ages. One man was so short that when he had to throw a grenade over some drilling. They had to take their rifles, tin hats and gas masks to work with them. When they arrived they were given a clip of bullets, which they handed in on their way home. The men worked six or sometimes even seven 12 hour shifts per week, as well as many hours training and doing guard duties. Dorothy Locke was one of five girls in the Thornycrofts Home Guard, doing signals. She says, 'They never put the girls in these photos!'

Above: After the bombing in Burgess Road, the houses on the left have lost their windows and some slates. The houses that were destroyed were behind the trees on the right of the picture. Some people in nearby Merton Road thought a bomb had landed in their garden. It turned out to be a mangle (younger readers may not know this was a heavy pair of rollers you pulled washing through to get the water out) which the bomb blast had blown from a Burgess Road house and dropped in their garden.

Above right: The Methodist church in Church Street was very badly damaged. The organ at the far end was completely destroyed. St Michael's church, opposite, lost all but one of its old stained-glass windows and the objects on the altar were blown around the church. The railings in the picture were later removed for the war effort. The sign points towards an air raid shelter. It was probably empty, as the air raid siren did not seem to have sounded.

Facing page: According to a newspaper article entitled 'THE YEAR IN RETROSPECT', this bombed house was in Church Lane. Workers are looking

through the rubble for any missing persons, and maybe smelling for gas leaks. The damaged houses were made safe later and local children used them to play in. On one occasion two boys set light to a mattress left behind, creating black smoke that got all over their hands and faces and brought them a good telling off from their parents.

A VE Day party in Brambly's Grange. People wondered if the second world war would ever end. But it did and on VE Day in May 1945, parties were held in thousands of towns and villages all over the country. Fine weather meant street parties. It can't have been easy to organise the food, as rationing carried on well into then 1950s. This one seems to be for the children and some soldiers home on leave, as well as servicemen from the plastic surgery unit at Rooksdown. Even on such a day, the people are all dressed up in hats and overcoats.

Another VE Day street party in 1945. This time it's mainly adults and it took place in May Street. May Street was knocked down in the 60s as part of the new road scheme and many door knockers and cast-iron fireplaces from these houses were collected for the museum.

Webbers, the car people

Today cars are everywhere and few homes are without at least one vehicle parked outside. But of course those who aspire to own a car must first find somewhere to buy one from. For the inhabitants of Basingstoke the car showrooms of choice are more often those belonging to WW Webber Ltd in New Road and Southern Road. But it is not only today's motorists who choose to buy their cars from Webbers - their parents, grandparents and even great grandparents could just as easily have bought a car there too.

Webbers, in fact, began business more than a century ago. Walter William Webber, the son of a railway worker moved to Basingstoke from the Oxford area in the late 19th century and took up a job as a grocer's assistant.

Walter soon gained a reputation as a keen amateur cyclist. His notoriety was enhanced by a report in the Hants & Berks Gazette. On April 2nd 1892 the paper

Right: *WW Webber moved from his home to live above these premises in Winchester Road in 1900. They were used in conjunction with the workshop in Victoria Street.* **Below:** *The Webber family on a day out in 1898.*

reported that Walter Webber and a friend had been charged with riding bicycles furiously so as to endanger the lives and limbs of foot passengers. Both men were fined seven shillings. Walter's reputation caused him to be frequently consulted by members of the public over their choice of cycle. Eventually he decided to stop giving free advice and start selling the machines himself. First two, then three and so on.

The bicycle business grew and expanded into motor vehicle maintenance. Around 1893 Walter Webber

THAT CAR REPAIR.
"SEE WEBBER
ABOUT IT"

Our Repair Works,
Entrance :- Southern Road.
PHONE 141.
W. W. WEBBER, LTD.
15 London St. Basingstoke.
AUSTIN & MORRIS SERVICE DEPÔT

opened a repair workshop in Jacob's Yard. In 1900 showroom premises were acquired in Winchester Street from where Walter sold bicycles, motor cycles and motor cars. The firm's founder chose this year as the official commencement date of the W Webber business.

In 1910 the business moved to London Street and was incorporated as WW Webber Ltd. By now motor vehicle sales and repairs were very much the main source of business. By 1913 the company was acting as agent for a number of different manufacturers including Ford, Studebaker, Singer, Morris Oxford, Austin and Wolsley.

The first world war had a dramatic effect on business, due to the acutely felt labour shortage, as more and more men at first volunteered for service in the forces or were later conscripted. Diversification became essential and so Walter Webber hired agricultural machinery to the Government becoming actively involved in the Tractor Ploughing Programme. Tragically, shortly after the war had ended, Walter's eldest son Morris died from illness on his homeward journey after service in India.

Top: W Webber's workshop in the old stables on Victoria Street, Basingstoke, circa 1900.
Above: An advert for Webbers from the 1930s.
Right: WW Webber outside his home in Cliddesden Road in 1955 with a Werner Motor Cycle. This is the same machine shown on the previous page in use on a Webber family outing.

Throughout the 1920s trading was poor due to the post war economic slump and the onset of the Great Depression. During this difficult period the Webber family consolidated its ownership of the business carrying its name. Walter Webber, the largest single shareholder, increased his stake and appointed his wife to the board. Their daughter Olive worked in the business as did their younger son Clifton Walter Webber. He was born in 1904 and started working for his father in his early teens as a direct result of the manpower shortages during the first world war. He was made a director of the firm in 1926, the year of the General Strike.

The economic depression continued into the 1930s but the business was in a comparatively good state and was able to capitalise on reduced property prices by acquiring a second set of premises in Alton. This was indeed the golden age of motoring when those

with cash could buy a twelve months old Austin Ten Saloon de luxe model for just £125. The Alton purchase was completed in 1933.

The venture was however never as successful as had been hoped and by 1939 the directors had begun to discuss the possibility of disposing of it. Then quite unexpectedly the business began to flourish and would do so throughout the war years.

Clifton Webber was already 35 when war had broken out but he decide to volunteer anyway; he was a good friend of the commanding officer at the nearby Bramley Camp and asked his advice. As a result of this advice Clifton applied to join the Royal Electrical and Mechanical Engineers, REME, and reported to the War Office in London.

As things turned out Clifton, however, never heard any more from the War Office. A few weeks after his interview in London an official from the Ministry of Supply contacted him in Basingstoke: it appears that the War Office had decided, that because of the nature of the business, Clifton was of more use to the country running WW Webber Ltd. What particularly appealed to the Ministry of Supply was the combination of maintenance and damage repair facilities. As a result, throughout the war the business was contracted to overhaul and repair military vehicles. As a consequence, as well as Clifton Webber, other key men

Both pictures: *Before and after. A Rover repaired by Webbers after colliding with a tank outside the gates of Hackwood Park during the second world war.*

in the company were also retained and the business did rather well. Work for the Ministry of Supply continued beyond the war's end and the prosperity it brought continued for the rest of the decade.

In 1932 Clifton Webber's son Roger Walter William Webber was born. In 1950 he joined the business as an apprentice. Part of his apprenticeship would include four years at Loughborough University training in general engineering. So began the career of the third generation of the Webber family to work in the family firm.

In common with the whole country the 1950s proved to be a very prosperous period for the company. Each year Webbers recorded satisfactory financial results. Although the directors had considered selling their Alton premises in 1939 they decided to persevere; indeed the outbreak of war made the sale impractical. Regrettably however Alton's performance continued to be disappointing and the premises there were finally sold in 1958.

The company's founder Walter William Webber died on 27th February 1960 at the age of 89 having witnessed astonishing changes to motor transport during the course of his long life, and to the business he had begun more than sixty years earlier.

Before the first world war Webbers had been agents for the various independent British motor manufacturers as well as American companies such as Ford and Studebaker. The intervening years saw the company concentrate on the British makes Austin, Morris, Riley, Wolseley, MG and Vanden Plas, names which would eventually evolve into BMC, the British Motor Corporation, in 1952.

In 1968 BMC merged with Rover, Triumph and Jaguar to form, initially, British Motor Holdings followed by what became British Leyland. Webbers continued to sell these vehicles throughout the fifties and sixties, adding Land Rover in 1964, and Jaguar in 1968, to its portfolio.

The post-war prosperity enjoyed in the 1950s continued into the next decade. Profits increased year on year until 1966 when rising inflation and selective employment tax made an impact. However the business did still grow during the decade with the erection of a new showroom and petrol facilities on Southern Road. Work started in 1963, and the showroom still exists today, now housing the company's Land Rover operation as well as the administration and accounts offices.

The 1970s saw major changes to the business. Before the second world war Basingstoke had been a small market town. After the war it was designated as a

London overspill town and new housing estates were built to accommodate the influx of people. In the mid 1960s the Borough Council initiated a major redevelopment of the town centre which would effect Webbers dramatically. Much of the old town was flattened to make way for a new shopping centre and multi-storey car park. London Street was pedestrianised and a new road was pushed right through the middle of Webbers' site.

Before that redevelopment Webbers had a long site stretching from Southern Road to London Street. A large proportion of the section from London Street to the new road was compulsorily purchased by the council along with land for the road itself. In return the council gave Webbers more land along its eastern and western boundaries leaving the firm with the site it presently occupies.

A new showroom was constructed on New Road together with a filling station. Brand new accounts and administration areas were created in what is now the Jaguar facility with new workshops being erected from north to south along the western boundary of the site. The Southern Road showroom then became a used car showroom. These extensive changes were completed by 1975.

Nationally the 1970s was a decade of high inflation and economic decline. Despite this the business remained largely profitable throughout those years even though severe doubts about the viability of the company's Leyland franchise were raised towards the end of that period.

Left: *An interesting assortment of vehicles being repaired in the workshop in the early 1950s.*
Below: *The first showroom in London Street, Basingstoke to which WW Webber moved from Winchester Street in 1910.*

Roger Webber had begun working full time in the business in 1956, after a period of national service. He soon demonstrated the same aptitudes as his father and grandfather and was made a director in 1960. By the early 1970s he was running the business and was made Managing Director in 1974. His father went into semi retirement but remained Chairman.

For Webbers the first half of the 1980s proved to be a period of consolidation and stability. The business was moderately profitable and no major site redevelopment was undertaken. The petrol pumps however were moved from the showroom side of New Road to the opposite side of the road where the now-redundant workshops had been situated. The surplus land was sold to the Post Office.

The second half of the decade proved much more eventful. British Leyland had evolved into Austin Rover and then Rover Cars under the ownership of British Aerospace. Despite new names and changes in ownership Rover continued to be plagued by reliability problems and it became harder and harder to make money despite ever increasing volumes of business.

Below: *The busy Bodyshop in the late 1950s.* ***Right:*** *The Southern Road showroom under construction in 1963.*

There were therefore doubts about the long term ability of the site to cope with Rover volumes which, coupled with profitability issues, eventually led the directors to relinquish Rover in favour of Honda in 1987. Jaguar and Land Rover however had been separated from Rover in 1980 and subsequently privatised; those marques were retained and moved to Southern Road showroom. Honda's volumes were one tenth of Rover's in 1987 and the restructuring allowed Webbers to remain on its existing site and still have a very profitable end to the decade.

Tragically Roger Webber died on 26th July 1989 from heart failure aged only 57. Roger's son Antony William Winton Webber (known as Winton) joined the business the same year aged 22. Winton's grandfather, Clifton

Webber, now forgetting all thoughts of a full retirement remained as Chairman.

The 1990s was an eventful decade for the business. The Land Rover franchise was growing rapidly with the introduction of the Discovery in late 1989. Jaguar Cars was bought by Ford and experienced four years of change. Honda did relatively well with the introduction of the Swindon-built Accord in 1992. A severe recession affected the whole country from mid 1990 onwards and was exacerbated with the Exchange Rate Mechanism crisis of 1992. Fortunately the Land Rover franchise remained strong during that difficult period and the company managed to weather the storm.

1994 saw new shoots of recovery. The new Jaguar XJ saloon was launched to critical acclaim and Webbers' Jaguar operation returned to profit. The Swindon-built Accord was now established in the fleet market and was soon to be joined by the five door Civic.

In 1995 the Honda facility was extensively refurbished and brand new work shops were added to the back. The accounts department was moved to new offices above the Southern Road showroom allowing the New Road frontage previously occupied to be converted into a brand new Jaguar showroom in time for the launch of the hugely successful XK8 range.

In 1997 the decision was taken to move Webbers' Bodyshop operation from workshops on Southern Road to a dedicated facility at the nearby Daneshill industrial estate. The relocation enabled the operation to expand dramatically. The area previously occupied by the

Bodyshop was then included as part of an extensive redevelopment of the Land Rover franchise which was competed in late 1998.

The year 2000 saw Webbers celebrate its official one hundredth birthday. Sadly Clifton Webber just failed to witness the celebrations, dying on 10th October 1999 at the ripe old age of 95. However, he lived long enough to see the management of the business pass to the fourth generation of the Webber family when his grandson Winton was made Joint Managing Director earlier that year.

Today Webbers is still owned by Walter Webber's direct descendants. The firm having now entered its second century the odds are high that the children, grand children and even great grand children of today's motorists may, like their forebears, still be buying their cars from WW Webber Ltd in another hundred years time.

Top: The 1974 refurbishment nears completion.
Above left: The Southern Road showroom in 1987. Below: An aerial view of Webber's New Road/Southern Road site as it is in the year 2000.

Carnival days

Left: London Street sees yet another Carnival Queen, Derrie Brennam from Essex Road. The first Carnival Queen was Miss Yvonne La Gogué, related to the Walkenshaw family at Bramley. Arthur Attwood used to help to count the votes for Carnival Queens: he says that if you were on a table for a popular entrant you had to work hard. Carnivals first started in 1937 and continued till 1939, to raise funds for the local hospital. They all made a profit. They were revived after the second world war. 1951 was the year of the Festival of Britain, one hundred years after the Great Exhibition of 1851, when our industrial nation boasted its greatness. At our carnival in Basingstoke there were events staged on every day from 7th to 14th July except Sunday. The procession took place on the Thursday, starting at 7 pm. The profits for 1951 were to restore the Deane's almshouses in London Street that are still in use

in the 21st century. The 1964 carnival had a newspaper called the Carnival Clarion. Its leading article was a send-up. The headline read, 'THE GRAND NATIONAL MAY COME TO BASINGSTOKE!' The 1967 paper had an even more bizarre headline, 'BASINGSTOKE BECOMES BRITAIN'S MOON SHOT BASE. TOWN PLAN ABANDONED!' Above the headline was a picture of a building site, with three rocket launch pads dominating the skyline!

Above: Cooking on a spit during the 1956 carnival. There is something strange about the picture. What is the cook looking at? Why is the boy standing there? Is he part of the demonstration? Perhaps he's first in the queue for the food. Hot Dogs not Hot Boys! Health regulations later caused this popular attraction to be dropped from the carnival events.

Monday night, during the Carnival Week, was Mardi Gras night, when the streets were closed for dancing and watching. A large crowd gathered, moving to the three dancing areas along London Street, outside the Town Hall and by the church. Each had a different style of dancing: modern, old-time and Latin American or jiving. Also on Mondays there was a cricket match at May's Bounty, the ground that Hampshire used for their county matches, although, alas, not any longer.

Those who did not want to dance, but do something more exciting, could enter the Grand Partner Whist Drive! Most days during the week, people could attend some sporting activity or show for people to attend in the War Memorial Park. One was called 'Have-a-go'

Archery. Edna Fielding says they used to have a game called 'Spot the Stranger'. You went all round the town, looking in the shop windows to find something the shopkeeper had put in that didn't belong, like a box of matches in a clothes shop.

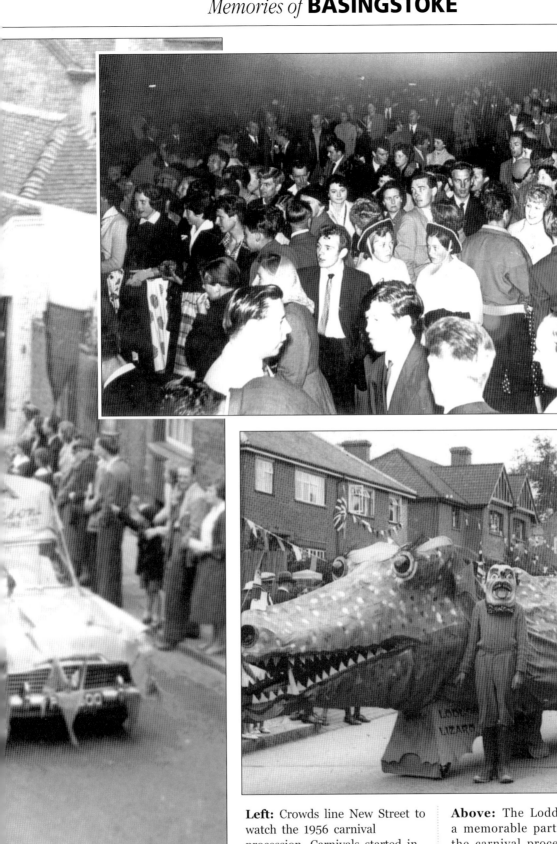

Left: Crowds line New Street to watch the 1956 carnival procession. Carnivals started in the late 1930s but, because of the war, they stopped and did not restart until 1951.Then there was a gap until 1956.The Queen in 1956 was Miss Jean Noyce. The profits were to be used to help build a community centre at Fairfields, the Carnival Hall. It was opened in 1964.

Above: The Lodden Lizzard, a memorable participant in the carnival procession.

Top: On the Saturday evening of Carnival Week, crowds would flock to the Memorial Park for the Grand Finale. There would be a mass bands march, ending with the Last Post and fireworks.

A 1960s fashion parade held in the Memorial Park during Carnival Week, organised by a local clothes shop. Dorothy Locke went on a fashion parade, wearing a dress and jacket of pale blue satiny material with spots on. She had made it herself, as you were supposed to, but she says a lot of entrants didn't! Fashion is the buzz word among all age groups today. Will any of these fashions ever come back? I expect some fashions have returned and some people have still got their sixties gear in the attic or maybe are still wearing them. There are teddy boys who hanker for the old days.

The town had two Carnival Queens. One a junior and the other not many years older. Contests were held and sometimes all the entrants' photographs appeared in the local paper. You can see the pair sitting at the end of the catwalk. The elder queen not taking much notice or making some remark to one of her attendants. 'I wouldn't be seen dead in that!' or 'that's my mum'.

Bottom: A Carnival Queen could go anywhere in the 60s. Here she is on the Town Hall balcony, watching the dancing in the streets below. This balcony has seen other more famous people speak from it. George Formby was up there once, but I don't know if he sang 'Leaning on a lamppost'. He was in Basingstoke to make the film; 'He Snoops to Conquer'. Yes, that right snoops not stoops.

Right: This is 1956, the year when anything could happen. Here, we see a boat on dry land. Is it a special hovercraft that cleans the roads at the same time? No, it's another float made for the procession that took place on Thursday during every Carnival Week. If there are any passengers, they are all inside, feeling roadsick, or left behind on the dock. Is anyone driving it? In fact, the float was made by Player's to advertise their cigarettes and the sailor was their well-

known sign. The float is making its way up New Street, past the original museum building that started life as the Mechanics Institute for adult learning and leisurely reading. Carnivals were an important part of the town's social life until 1994. There was a great deal of ingenuity in the designing and building of floats and the dressing of 'walking entries'.

Shopping spree

This picture was taken in 1958 on one of the two market days, Wednesday or Saturday. There was always a policeman on duty during market days. They did four-hour shifts, starting at 6 am and went on until 10 pm. Strong arms and feet and a calm patient nature were obviously needed for this task. One such policeman was Dennis Padwick who was here between the years 1936 and 1950, doing a further stint in the town 1964 to 1966 as Superintendent. So, we know he is not the bobby on duty in this picture!

There had long been a chemist's on the site of Whites & Taylors. It started off as Meatyard & Sapp around the 1850s and sold items such as vermifuge electuary, rhubarb and ginger pills, laxative pills, the 'female pill', camphoric vegetable tooth powder, the stomach and chest plaster, itch ointment and cleansing worm powders. They also provided approved trusses for every kind of rupture and gave advice. They sold philosophical incense lamps and ambrosial pastilles for fumigating rooms and imparting a delightful fragrance. The shop name changed from Meatyard & Sapp to Arkas Sapp. Timothy White's & Taylor, one of a chain of chemists, was there in 1907. After moving to the new shopping precinct, they were bought out by Boots the Chemist.

Both pictures: Potter's Lane linked Church Street with Wote Street. It was full of shops in the 1940s. You could buy milk, wallpaper, baby prams and fish, among many other items. One shop that was well known around Hampshire was the Southern Counties Cycle Co. It was a wooden and corrugated iron shed with a chalk floor and no heating and it was full of bicycles and spare parts! It was run by Charlie Everett. His mechanics worked upstairs and he would call up to them with instructions. They assembled bicycles and put on their own badge, the 'Southern Counties Cycle Company'. They sold good bicycles, according to Ron Fletcher, who bought one from the shop. 'It cost my father £4.1Os, I think,' he said. This was some time in the 1920s. In 1939 Arthur Attwood bought a Hercules for just over £5. He says, 'It was a good bicycle that took me to Hatfield in Hertfordshire on nine weekends, 60 miles there and 60 miles back.' Dorothy Locke remembers going into the shop and 'seeing bikes strung to the ceiling on meat hooks' so that they could be worked on from below. She goes on to say that Charlie knew how to cadge them from Mr Howe, the butcher, whose shop was across the street. You could get your puncture mended by one of Charlie's mechanics or park your bike there for twopence a day and know that it was safe. All these shops in Potter's Lane closed down to make way for the new shopping centre in 1966.

Winnie and Ruby Philpott were the daughters of Charles Philpott (Winnie, the eldest, is on the left here and Ruby on the right). When he came to Basingstoke in 1898, he opened a shop in Potter's Lane and he and his family lived over it. Charles baked bread and a variety of fancy cakes. The atmosphere in the shop was friendly and busy. Lily, his wife, and Winnie served in the shop. Ruby said that she herself was a lazy person but her sister Winnie was good in the shop because she was such a nice person. During the first year, Charles placed a wedding cake in a sealed round glass case in the shop window. That cake, once kept in Ruby's attic, is now over 100 years old and is on display in the town's Willis Museum. During the 1930s the world went through a terrible economic depression, with many people out of work and money scarce. Charles began to sell stale cakes, three for the price of one. He also allowed people to bring in their meals to be cooked in his ovens, so the families didn't need to light their cooking stoves and it saved them fuel. He charged a penny each time. Delivery boys took round orders in baskets and for special occasions, such as wedding and dances, the boys pushed a handcart. Charles died in 1935 but his family carried on the business. When Lily died in 1958, the two sisters carried on the work. Ruby was a music teacher and never really enjoyed serving in the shop, though she did at times. Winnie knew how to treat her customers and would always take her time serving people, making them feel that they were special. They had to give up the shop in 1964. Two years later it had gone, pulled down because of the town development. It must have been a sad day for Ruby and Winnie as they watched a life-time's work crash to the ground. Winnie died in 1979 and Ruby in 1999.

Down at the bottom of New Street was this imposing 'art deco' building. Kenneth Reed's was established in 1937 and closed in 1978. Mr Reed, who owned and ran the shop, was both a chemist and a photographer. He died in March 1990. David Smith ran the Milk Bar next door. This opened in 1950 and sold many flavoured milk shakes. You could say it was the 'MacDonald's' of its day in the town! It was bright and cheerful. Milk shakes tasted of chocolate, banana, strawberry and coffee. 'You sat on high stools at the bar, which didn't encourage you to stay long!' Staff and postmen from the Post Office up the street also frequented the Milk Bar. This block in New Street was called Queen's Parade and was built in 1933 for local traders by H J Goodall, the Basingstoke builders. Before the Parade was built, the site was occupied by an old house and gardens. The chemist's was opposite a doctors' surgery. People waiting for a prescription could get a drink at the milk bar or buy tobacco and sweets at the other shop nearby.

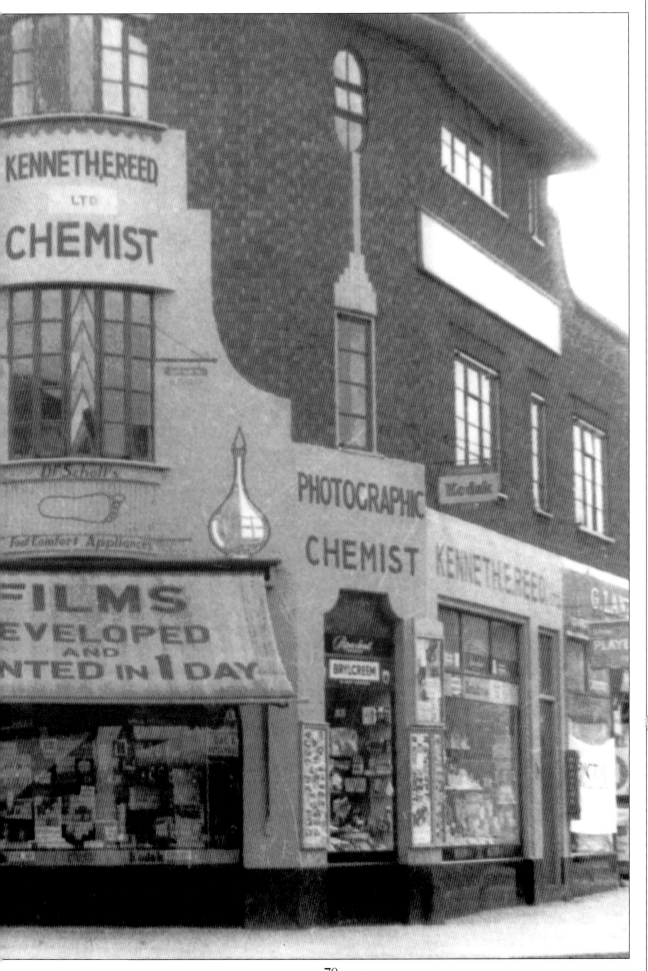

Making a living

The Goldings Park Motor Co Ltd in London Road opened in the 1920s and supplied 'Fordson tractors, implements, cars, vans and trucks'. They also repaired vehicles, using Ford trained mechanics, according to their advert in the 1951 Carnival programme. Their phone number was 241, which shows how few phones there were in the town. It closed about the end of the 1940s, though a car showroom occupies that site at the time of writing.

As you go down London Road from its junction with London Street, New Street and Hackwood Road, you come across a house known as Goldings on the right hand side. This was once purchased by Thomas Burberry, so that when the Town Council had enough money they could buy it as additional civic offices. The parkland behind the house became the Memorial Park. Further down is the White Hart inn and up Crossborough Hill is a school that started as a Girl's High School in Brook House, moved to Crossborough Hill and later took the name of its first headmistress, Harriet Costello. Then comes the Common, where people could graze their animals by ancient right. This area is used today for a variety of activities, such as dog walking, vintage car shows and car parking for events in the Memorial Park. The Common has now been moved east of the Ring Road to the land between Basingstoke and Old Basing.

The Telephone Exchange, just off New Street, had the human touch, with a friendly voice asking which number you required. The night supervisor, here in the picture, was Mr Albert Bell. A good name for a telephone worker! The exchange was demolished in 1979 and an automatic exchange was opened in Victoria Street. The first telephone exchange operated from an upper room above Mr Flux's shop at 62 Wote Street in about 1900. Henry A Flux was a clothier and hosier. He sold 'smart up-to-date goods' in 1916. 'We are noted for shirts, collars and ties and headgear,' reads one of his adverts. In old trade directories, telephone numbers are in the hundreds, not the thousands as they are today.

Above: Buses passing in Winchester Street in 1963. There is barely room for these two buses to pass each other. This corner is still narrow today, but after police officers had done point duty there for some years, traffic lights were put up to control the traffic.

Top: Looking down Victoria Street towards Winchester Street, showing the Venture Bus Depot. Venture Limited launched its first services on 5 May 1926, at the time of the General Strike. There was one service between Basingstoke and Overton, and another was an 'emergency' service between Basingstoke and Reading. This was a substitute for the GWR train services, which were cancelled because of the strike. During the early years the area served extended to the villages and towns between Basingstoke, Newbury, Reading, Hartford Bridge, Andover, Stockbridge, Alton, Alresford and Winchester, as well as local services in and around Basingstoke. However, many of these services operated only a few days a week and several of the longer routes were soon abandoned. The business was initially operated from premises in Reading Road, but in 1929 a new garage was opened in Victoria Street and remained the headquarters of the company until its take-over by Red and White United Transport Limited in 1945. The buses continued to run under the Venture name until a further take-over by Wilts and Dorset in 1950. Mafeking House on the right was named for the Relief of Mafeking in the Boer War. Here, in their Victoria Street salesrooms, Aston and Company sold a variety of second-hand furniture. In 1937 you could get a piano for 70 shillings and a child's cot for 10 shillings. They made leather goods such as handbags at the back of the shop. Articles were also made by outworkers in their own homes: gas mask cases, shopping bags and tea cosies, for something like 2d for 50. Dorothy Locke says, 'I tried it once. I only did one bag and it nearly ruined my machine. You needed a big treadle machine.' For the Coronation of George VI, Mr Aston produced hundreds of banners reading 'LONG MAY THEY REIGN' and sold them all over the country. Arthur Attwood says that Mundays, where they were printed onto fabric, must have used gallons of ink.

Both pictures: What were they doing on the Town Hall roof? They were taking down the clock tower that had stood on the Town Hall since 1887. The cast iron supports were cracking and it had to come down. They discovered this in November 1960 and the men on the roof were there in 1961, taking it apart.

The shop that you can see is Kingdons. It started life in 1853 as an ironmonger's. Here it is called a hardware store, selling all kinds of useful household items. Kate Webb described the shop as a 'little sort of nuts and bolts and nails shop. I remember the sound and smell, the sound of the wooden slatted floorboards, they were sort of splintery-looking, rather dull, the brown counter and the browny-grey overalls that the men used to wear that served there. But you could buy anything there, any nuts and bolts, any household do-it-yourself items.'

Rawlings Transport

The need to move goods from one place to another has been with us since commerce and trade began. Back packs, pack horses, and dug-out canoes would give way to great wooden ships, caravans of camels and eventually to railways and steamships. And in our own times, still within living memory, the road and road transport would become king with fleets of lorries driven by new knights of the road taking goods along the economic arteries of Britain, keeping our shops and factories filled with the goods and products we need.

To meet the increase demand for road haulage during the latter half of the 20th century, many privately owned road haulage companies would spring up, some briefly and then disappear from our memories, others more robust, would thrive, gradually making us aware that they are here to stay.

Edward Rawlings (Hook) Limited was founded by Edward Rawlings senior who was from a London family, which had moved to Hook in the 1940s to become meat dealers and cattle slaughterers, selling and delivering mainly to pet food shops including his own in Aldershot and Farnham. After the morning run,

the van that was used for the shop deliveries, would sit idle - but not for long.

Rawlings Transport was launched in 1972 by Edward Terry Rawlings who used the van in the afternoons to deliver boxes of nails locally and nationwide for a Basingstoke manufacturer. The company's reputation for reliability and service started with this first contract and word spread to companies such as Lansing Bagnall Ltd, which used the van for urgent small deliveries. Their requirement for larger vehicles prompted Terry to invest in heavy goods vehicles and with this, the company began to grow, attracting customers from all over Basingstoke and Hampshire.

Growth has been achieved by providing UK and European road haulage, and as technological advances have occurred in the Basingstoke area, Rawlings Transport has developed services to meet their requirements.

The computer and electronics industries, for example, have made it necessary to supply equipment that allows

Below: *An early Rawlings vehicle.*

for gentle handling of the most demanding and delicate products such as cameras and recording equipment for Sony BPE who use Rawlings Specialised Movements Division for the transportation and installation of their studios (including Big Brother) all over Europe.

During Operation Desert Storm following the Iraqi invasion of Kuwait, the firm was appointed by the USAF to transport bombs from RAF Welford to Newport Docks for shipment to Allied bases in Saudi Arabia. This operation went on 24 hours a day throughout the conflict using virtually all the firm's trucks.

Then in 1993, Rawlings Fuels was formed to supply domestic heating oil througout the area. Using the sales expertise of Ken Humphreys the company now has over 7,000 domestic and commercial customers, all of who use Rawlings Fuels for its high level of service and competitive pricing.

The Heating Service Department complements this by offering advice and service on any boiler maintenance problem, or tank replacement.

The group of companies grew further with the opening of the Specialised Movements Division in 1998. This was started to cover every aspect of delivering goods from

Above: *A Rawlings tanker.* ***Left and top:*** *Two of the company's fleet.*

emergency water tankering to the installation of machines using vehicle mounted cranes, along with computer and electronics installations using state of the art vehicles.

However, throughout this expansion, the mainstay is still the UK Road Transport Department, which operates over 40 vehicles delivering goods on behalf of such high street names as Brita Water Filter Systems, Bacardi Martini, Gillette, Thames Water, SSI Schaefer and still Lansing Linde after all these years.

Rawlings have a policy of purchasing top of the range new vehicles, these vehicles with their distinctive blue, red and yellow colours and registration numbers ending in the suffix RAW can be spotted throughout Europe, advertising not only the company but also the customer, several of whom have the trailers painted in their own livery.

With a staff of over 60 employees, Rawlings is still growing and committed to the high level of service the company was built on. At the time of writing (Autumn 2000) the turnover is expected to exceed £6m.

After more than a quarter of a century, Terry Rawlings remains at the firm's head as its Managing Director, together with Company Directors - John Rawlings, Mary Stent, Paul Rawlings and Tracy Wells.

The Rawlings family employs a hands-on approach to running the business and that personal touch is undoubtably one of the major factors in its success.

Above: *One of Rawlings modern fleet of vehicles.*
Below: *Vehicles in customers' livery.*

'Ave a banana!

Bananas are a part of the British culture. For many years prior to the arrival of the large supermarkets, towns like Basingstoke had their own little banana depot down by the railway line. Things have changed a little since then but the banana is still Britain's favourite fruit. The banana plant is indigenous to Southern Asia and Indochina and was first reported in Europe by Marco Polo, who sampled his first banana at the court of Kublai Khan. Plants were, however, eventually taken westward by Arab merchants to Africa and from there, by Portuguese explorers, to the Canary Islands and by later adventurers to the Caribbean and the Americas. In the 1880s there were regular if small shipments to London and Liverpool. In Liverpool bananas were being imported from the Canaries by Elder Dempster. In September 1888 Edward Wathen Fyffe, a London-based Scottish merchant, decided to supplement his family tea importing business by receiving a very small quantity of bananas at his office in Howford Buildings in Fenchurch Street, London. He had 'discovered' bananas in the Canary Islands after taking his sick wife there to convalesce some time earlier. The bananas were sold at Covent Garden.

By 1895 EW Fyffe, Son & Co Fruit Growers and Importers were being referred to in the press as the largest banana merchants in Europe.

Fyffe's major rival at that time, Elder Dempster, began importing bananas from Jamaica in refrigerated ships in 1901. This technique made it possible to ship bananas half way around the world more successfully and, seeing the potential benefits, Fyffes organised a merger with Elder Dempster later that same year.

The following year 45 per cent of Elders & Fyffes was acquired by the United Fruit Company of America; the injection of capital enabled the company to source bananas from many more countries.

In 1904 the Fyffes banana boat passenger services began and the future looked rosy. In 1914 Elders & Fyffe however became wholly owned by United Fruit - though it did the owners little good when supplies were terminated by the first world war.

Above centre: Advertising in the 1930s.
Below and facing page, top: A delivery van from the late 1920s.

In 1929 the emergence of the Jamaican Banana Producers Association provided a new level of competition as a counter to which Fyffes introduced the Fyffes Blue Label. The sticky label ensured that Fyffe's bananas could be readily identified by retailers and their customers alike.

Why did bananas disappear so rapidly from our shops at the outbreak of the second world war? The main answer is that Fyffes' vessels were requisitioned by the government. Many people date the real end of the war to the day when they next saw bananas in the shops. On 30th December 1945 Fyffes brought the first commercial shipment of bananas since 1939, 10 million of them, into Avonmouth harbour aboard the SS Tilapa.

Many other changes have occurred in the industry since refrigerated shipping began in 1901: in 1961 for example bananas began being shipped in cartons rather than in wooden boxes, whilst in 1972 Fyffes ripening centres were rationalised and modernised. A further important change occurred in 1979 when Fyffes bananas ceased to be carried by rail as the developing motorway system offered a more efficient and economical transport method.

Above: *The first advertising campaign from 1929.*
Right: *Fyffes' premises today.*

At the end of the day however the Fyffes business has been about selling more bananas. In 1984 Fyffes helped to set up The Banana Group to generically promote and advertise bananas; that year 300,000 tonnes of bananas were imported into the UK. The project was immensely successful: by the end of the century 750,000 tonnes of bananas were being imported into the UK annually - consumption had doubled in ten years.

Before then however, in 1986, Fyffes Group Ltd was acquired by Fruit Importers of Ireland becoming FII Fyffes for a little while before finally becoming Fyffes PLC in 1990.

Over the decades Fyffes has branched out into many areas of business which now encompasses 175 lines of fruit and 130 lines of vegetables - even so it is Fyffes' bananas with their famous blue label which remain every family's favourite.

The motorist's friend

The Automobile Association, to most of us simply The AA, is now a much respected British institution with a major presence in the town.

The Association was founded on 29th June 1905 by a group of motorists who met at London's Trocadero restaurant. The Association's first aim was to help motorists avoid police speed traps which were then catching motorists who exceeded the recently imposed 20 mph speed limit. The original few members of 1905 grew to 83,000 by 1914.

In 1906 the AA erected the country's first effective danger and warning signs on roads, and continued to provide sign posts until that became the responsibility of local authorities in the 1930s.

The first AA Members' Handbook appeared in 1908 and the following year the AA introduced its free legal defence service for drivers summoned to magistrates courts.

In 1910 the first AA routes were introduced with hand written route details provided to members - by 1929 239,000 were being issued annually. Today the AA produces ten million books a year. From 1912 the AA also started to inspect hotels and those receiving the famous star classification were included in the AA

Handbook. By the early 1920s car pre-purchase and post-accident repair checks were introduced.

By the outbreak of the second world war in 1939 there were two million cars on Britain's roads and 725,000 members of the AA. At the end of the war the AA led the protests against continuing petrol rationing, which was finally lifted in 1950. In recent years the AA has lobbied successive governments over unfair motoring taxes and the lack of investment in transport.

The introduction of two way radio after the second world war saw the 1949 launch of a night-time breakdown service in the London area, a service which was gradually extended to cover the whole country. Although the AA began selling motor insurance in 1907 - 23 years before such insurance became compulsory - it did not establish its own insurance underwriting service until 1967. Today AA Insurance is the UK's largest motor insurance intermediary whilst personal loans and instalment payment facilities are available through AA Financial Services.

Above left: *A 1930s motor-cycle patrolman.*
Right: *The erection of an early AA roadsign.*
Below: *Her Majesty the Queen opening Fanum House, Basingstoke in 1973.*

other businesses to achieve excellent financial returns and to re-establish the AA as the motorists' organisation.

In 1998 the AA reduced its call-to-arrival time at a breakdown to just 35 minutes, nearly ten minutes faster than in 1997. The following year the AA announced that it was pulling out of its retail network of 142 shops, insurance underwriting and home assistance services. Other changes which occurred in 1999 included the centralisation of its deployment operations at three supercentres in Halesowen, Thatcham and Cheadle.

Motor cycle combinations for AA patrols, introduced from 1920 together with roadside telephones, had been replaced by four-wheeled vehicles by 1968. Solo motor cycles were reintroduced in 1973 to combat urban congestion. In 1973 AA Relay was introduced, guaranteeing to transport any seriously broken down vehicle together with its occupants to any destination in Britain. That same year also saw the AA move its headquarters from London's Leicester Square, an area where it had occupied premises since 1929, to Fanum House in Basingstoke which was opened by Her Majesty the Queen in 1973.

Most importantly, in June 1999 Centrica, the leading supplier of energy and services to homes in Great Britain, announced its bid to buy the AA for £1.1 billion. The sale was completed in September after members voted overwhelmingly in favour.

AA Roadwatch, Europe's largest traffic broadcaster, came into being in 1973 with the advent of commercial radio in the UK.

In June 2000 the AA's pre-eminence in providing a roadside service was confirmed when it was named in independent research as the UK's top ranked roadside assistance provider for the second year running.

In 1990 the AA Driving School was launched which today has more than 1,000 franchisees. Two years later AA membership reached a record eight million, a figure which would rise to 10 million by the end of 2000.

The AA's founders could never have dreamed that their simple association to beat speed traps would one day grow so large and influential.

Towards the close of the decade, in 1997, the AA reviewed its activities, committing itself to three main objectives: to be pre-eminent at the roadside, to manage its portfolio of

Above left: *AA patrols saluted motorists unless there was a speed trap up ahead.* ***Above right:*** *The first UK roadside petrol station was run by the AA.* ***Below:*** *A modern AA patrol comes to the rescue of a Basingstoke motorist near the Leisure Centre.*

From 200 students to over 200 courses

The Basingstoke Technical Institute opened in the old Grammar School building in Worting Road, which had been used during the war by the Bank of England. Initially the Institute was the only further education organisation in Hampshire, pre-dating the formation of Farnborough Technical College in 1956. As a result, the Basingstoke Technical Institute provided training for most of the county, including the British Railways works at Eastleigh and as late as 1970 for training organisations as far afield as Fareham. The creation of Eastleigh and Fareham Colleges enabled the Basingstoke Technical Institute to focus on training and education in North Hampshire.

Basingstoke College of Technology now has over 200 courses. Choose from Management Studies, Travel and Tourism, Fashion and Textiles or even Small Animal Care.

In September 1948 Basingstoke Technical Institute opened its doors to two hundred students, most of whom were Thorneycroft apprentices in engineering. The courses were described as 'day classes in engineering and building'. Since then the School of Engineering has developed into a comprehensive package of Electronic, Mechanical, Manufacturing and Sound Engineering courses, holding true to the original purpose of the College whilst continuing to expand the range of courses offered. By 1951 the Institute had existed for five years funded

Right: *The newly built college in 1960.* **Below:** *The General Studies Department, staff and students in 1960.*

by Hampshire Local Education Authority, but without a Principal. A mildly critical HMI report stimulated the LEA to appoint J Neville Bradley as the first Principal, a post he held for 21 years. By 1954 student numbers had grown to over seven hundred, a significant number of those were in the new areas of office studies and catering, and the Institute changed its name to Basingstoke Technical College.

In 1960 the first phase of new buildings on the south side of Worting Road, on the site of corporation allotments, was opened by Queen Elizabeth II; and ten years later a second building, connected to the first was also opened. BCOT's second Principal, Robin Higgs succeeded Neville Bradley in 1973. He was succeeded by Steve Cowser, the current Principal, in 1988 when the College became Basingstoke College of Technology. Between 1988 and 2000 the college has seen extraordinary growth, almost doubling the number of students to 1,900 full time and 8,000 part

Arthur Gamble

Arthur Gamble

Arthur Gamble

time students. In 1996 the College opened its new building, on the site of the old grammar school in which the original classes were held. Princess Anne officially opened the building.

From its Engineering beginnings in 1948, Hampshire's first College has transformed into an educational centre of excellence for a wide range of subjects. Basingstoke College of Technology now offers a wide variety of training opportunities with innovative methods of delivery by 15 schools of study. There is a 'state-of-the-art' Information and

Learning Technology facility which allows students to study on-line or with multimedia. Many programmes are delivered in the workplace or in the five Community Learning Centres in and around Basingstoke (all of which provide free computer tuition for the community at times to suit the customer). Training and education have never been so flexible or accessible.

Top: A bricklayers outing to Brighton in 1962.
Left: *Apprentice bricklayers in 1962.* ***Right:*** *HRH Princess Royal opening the North Site building in 1996.* ***Below:*** *The main entrance of the North Site Building.* ***Below left:*** *ILT classes, 2000.*

Your very good health

'By Appointment to HM the Queen and the Prince of Wales Wine and Spirit Merchants'. That's the proud boast of the long-established firm of Berry Bros & Rudd with its shop, cellars and warehouse at Houndmills, Basingstoke.

Led by Christopher Berry Green, who would become the company's chairman in July 2000, the world famous wine merchants Berry Bros & Rudd built their temperature controlled wine warehouse in Basingstoke in 1967. The large site is on the now quiet Hamilton Close, though the road was previously the busy A339 main Newbury road. Since being built the firm's premises on the Houndmills estate have been greatly extended to include a bonded section built in the 1970s, additional offices, a modern tasting room and a retail shop in the old bottling hall. The total capacity is around 160,000 cases including 25,000 cases held in storage on behalf of customers. Despite these large numbers the computer-aided stock handling and despatch systems allow the work of this vast building to be managed by only a handful of people.

The Basingstoke building opened in May 1967 to store all the company's wines, port and whisky which had previously been housed in eight different locations in London. Bottling continued in Basingstoke until the early 1990s when producers insisted on bottling at source. One of the biggest growth areas in the 1990s has been the wine broking side of the business, with most of the output being as exports to the Far East and the USA. Ever pioneers in the wine trade, today the company sells wine by mail order and over the Internet. Six vans are now used to deliver throughout a fifty mile radius.

Basingstoke was initially only a bottling, storage and distribution warehouse. A retail facility was opened in a converted office in the 1970s to be followed in 1995 by the present superb shop facilities where there is also an impressive fine food section.

Although also operating duty free shops at Heathrow's Terminal Three and Four and businesses in Dublin, Hong Kong and Tokyo, the firm's main premises are at 3 St James's Street in London. The business has occupied those premises since the 1690s, an astonishing record. Even more astonishing is that eight generations of the same family should have been involved in the business from the mid 18th century to present times.

The Royal Warrant made its welcome appearance in 1903 after many years of association with the Royal Household. In 1923 the firm was chosen to furnish the wine cellar of Queen Mary's famous Dolls House now at Windsor castle. Everything was made exactly to scale, each miniature bottle containing exactly what was written on the label: there

Top left: The first George Berry, 1787-1854. Above right: Hugh Rudd. Far right: The new wine and fine food shop situated in the old bottling hall. Right: Anthony Berry in his robes of office as Master of the Vintners' Company.

merchanting family, RG Rudd and Son of Norwich. Hugh Rudd joined the then partners in the firm, cousins Walter and Francis Berry, as junior partner. The business became a limited company in 1943, taking its present name, with Hugh Rudd as chairman to be followed by Anthony Berry in 1965, John Rudd in 1985 and Christopher Berry Green in 2000.

How many other small firms, we wonder, have achieved such outstanding success in the modern world whilst retaining the essential elements of a family firm: personal service, knowledge and integrity? After more than three hundred years of trading Berry Bros & Rudd is surely the best in the business!

Top left: Bottling port from the wood. **Left:** *John Rudd, who was Chairman from 1985 until 2000.* **Below:** *Christopher Berry Green, the firm's current Chairman.* **Bottom:** *Berrys' premises at Houndmills, Basingstoke.*

were 38 different wines and even a miniature cellar book with a complete record of the stock.

In the same year that the Dolls House was completed, the firm also made history of another kind by introducing its now world-renowned brand of blended scotch whisky: Cutty Sark. The label for the brand was drawn by the famous Scottish artist James McBey who decided that the hand drawn lettering should spell out the contents' name as 'Scots' whisky rather than the usual Sassenach 'Scotch'; the distinctive yellow background to the label came about as a printer's error but was so striking that the firm decided to keep it.

Today there are huge stacks of the firm's Cutty Sark whisky stored in Scotland awaiting shipment to all parts of the world.

The name of the firm has changed over the years with the involvement of the Pickering, Clarke, Browne, Berry and Rudd families down the decades. The name Berry Bros & Rudd made its appearance only during the second world war long after Hugh Rudd joined the firm. The 'brothers' in the firm's name go back to 1854 when George Berry, the then sole proprietor, died leaving the business to his two sons George and Henry.

Hugh Rudd joined the firm of Berry Bros in 1920 the scion of another wine

Turning millions to billions

When a company's assets on its balance sheet are about £7 thousand million pounds one is talking very big business indeed.

And Basingstoke's Winterthur Life UK Holdings Ltd based on Winterthur Way really does have assets on that extraordinary scale.

Winterthur Life is the UK Life Assurance and Pensions arm of the Winterthur Swiss Insurance Group which is in turn part of Credit Suisse, one of the largest asset managers in the world.

Winterthur UK however can trace its origins back to the London of late 19th century when the business was founded by Baron Profumo. For over a century the firm was known as Provident Life and pioneered the concept of buying homes linked to life assurance.

'The Provident' was founded on 3rd October 1877 by Baron Profumo, an Italian born of a Genoese family though educated in England. Baron Profumo had early recognised the importance of linking life assurance to mortgages, but it would take his fledgling company 12 years to accumulate the £200,000 then needed to provide the legal minimum deposit necessary to establish a life insurance subsidiary - the Provident Free Home Life Assurance Co Ltd.

From the outset the company provided a way into home ownership for ordinary people who could not normally afford to put down a deposit. A policy holder who paid premiums of half a crown (12 ½ p) a week for five years however earned the right to borrow the whole price of a house costing £250. The repayments were then 7s 6d (37 ½ p) a week, less than the cost of renting a house - and after 25 years the house would be paid for.

Expansion continued and by 1889 the company had outgrown its original premises in Lombard Street. New premises, Provident House, were acquired in 'Bishopsgate Street Without' to house the firm's two hundred staff. There the provision of

mahogany desks, counter and fittings were taken for granted as were high stools and desks. Also provided were the latest in technology with not only speaking tubes but their short lived successors the 'electrical speaking tube' and electric lights. Observing the social proprieties of the times female staff were provided with a separate entrance to the building.

By 1902 more than half a million pounds a year was being lent with house prices averaging £325.

Baron Profumo died suddenly in 1911 but Provident Life still stayed in the Profumo family's ownership.

Top left: Baron Profumo, founder of 'The Provident'. **Above centre:** *An early 20th century picture of the Provident building.*

New premises were needed following the end of the second world war. It took until 1967 before building work could commence on new offices - a new Provident House near Spitalfields Market where Provident Life, together with its subsidiary United Standard Insurance, could be housed. The new building would become known as 'the Silver Tower' in the City of London because of its stainless steel cladding and solar grey glass windows.

Provident Life was acquired by Winterthur in 1981. Four years later the company moved to Basingstoke where it now employs 550 of its 850 staff. The company changed its name to Winterthur Life in 1995 to reflect its Swiss parentage.

During the 1990s the company enjoyed a growth rate in new business of one thousand per cent.

By the end of the 1990s the company would be showing a return on capital of 30 per cent, business had increased by 11 per cent in the last year of the decade with a 75 per cent increase in group personal pensions plans and with assets under management having increased threefold to £2.3 billion between 1995 and 1999.

At the close of the decade the company acquired another business, Colonial Life UK,

for a purchase price of £301 million. The combined business increased Winterthur's assets under management to almost £7 billion propelling the company into the Top 30 insurers, by gross premiums written, and increasing the company's customers to 600,000.

Since moving to Basingstoke in 1985 the company has sponsored Basingstoke Railway Station, recently assisting with the installation of CCTV and installing signs proclaiming 'Welcome to Basingstoke - the Home of Winterthur Life'. The company also sponsors the Anvil concert hall and the Milestones Museum as well as being a major contributor to local charities.

Business really is big in Basingstoke!

Above: *The company's advert for its home ownership scheme.*
Right: *Winterthur Life today.*

Riding the waves

There can hardly have been a woman in Britain born since the end of Queen Victoria's reign who has not had a perm or had her hair dyed at some time or another; and when she did the chances are that she made use of a Wella hair care product.

Wella is Germany's largest - and the world's second largest - producer of hairdressing products for home and professional use. The company's international headquarters are located in Darmstadt near Frankfurt from where the world wide Wella Group is administered.

The company's beginnings can be traced back to 1880 when 26 year old Franz Ströher, the great grandfather of today's generation of owners founded a company called Franz Ströher-Rothenkirchen in Rothenkirchen to produce and distribute artificial hair for wigs and hairpieces.

By the mid 1920s the permanent waving technique invented by Frenchman Francois Marcel in 1872 had been improved and Wella acquired a licence to manufacture a range of easy to use permanent wave machines. The company was soon also producing hair dryers and salon equipment.

In 1924 the brand name Wella (German for Wave) was registered and the world's first pointwind permanent waving system was launched.

Wella equipment first came to Britain in the 1920s although the British Wella company was not formed until 1932 when two unemployed men, Jack Carlton and Leo Hartman,

formed Wella Rapid Ltd with just £100, their object being importing and selling the Wella permanent waving machines, lotions and other accessories.

It would take many years however for the British business to expand from two men in a dingy back room in Bloomsbury to the current 400 plus employees in one of Britain's largest and most modern hair care headquarters at Basingstoke with a turnover of more than £85 million.

The tiny British company soon moved to 5/6 Eden Street just north of Euston Road. Eden Street was lost in the redevelopment of the 1960s but remained Wella's UK headquarters until 1962.

Wella Rapid's first British advertisement appeared in the Hairdressers' Journal in January 1933 and slowly the business began to grow. By 1935 the Wella Junior Pointwind Machine would cost hairdressers the substantial sum of £49 10s, whilst the cost of a perm to clients was then typically between 10/6d and 15s - but Wella did claim the perm would last for nine months. The products became immensely popular.

So successful did the company become that a branch was opened in Leeds in 1938 to take care of northern sales - sales which were soon to dwindle as trade with Germany ceased for the duration of the second world war.

Business soon recovered however in the post-war years. The period between 1959 and 1967 was one of remarkable growth for Wella. In these eight years the company's British sales increased more than seven-fold. Wella operated eight tuition

Top left: *Franz Ströher, founder of Wella.* **Above centre:** *An early advertisement for Wella's products.*
Right: *The factories and laboratories at Rothenkirchen in the 1930s.*

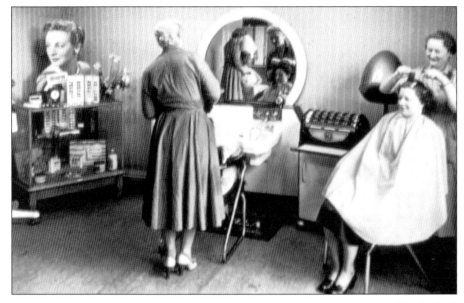

green field site (since extended to four acres) at Basingstoke with the appropriate address of Wella Road. A year later a new factory was opened in Pontyclun in South Wales to cope with the ever increasing demand for Wella Products.

The company name Wella Rapid Ltd which had survived since 1932 was now changed to Wella (Great Britain) Ltd reflecting a new forward looking business offering many more hair products than simply those concerned with perms. The 1970s was a decade during which the company would launch many new hair care products for both salon and home use.

To support ever expanding sales an impressive new Southern Distribution Centre was opened in Basingstoke in 1986 with 55,000 sq ft of space where over 6,000 pallets could be stored, nearly three times the previous capacity.

During the 1990s Wella's expansion continued through the acquisition of such names as Vosene, Silvikrin, Bristows and the Shaders and Toners brands bought from SmithKline Beecham, whilst Wella launched its own Viva Long Lasting Colour, the first ever reversible home hair colouring product.

centres, and half a million pounds was being spent annually on technical tuition for hairdressers.

In one single month in 1967 sales would top the total annual sales of just eight years earlier.

In 1962 the company transferred its head office operation to new headquarters built on a 2.5 acre

Now, at the dawn of a new millennium, Wella successfully continues to bring the latest products and technical innovations in hair care to an ever more discerning public.

Top: *A Wella tuition centre in the 1950s.*
Above left: *A Wella sponsored hairdressing competition in 1959.* ***Below:*** *Wella's Basingstoke headquarters in 1962.*

Kings of culture

The world we live in contains countless small germs or bugs. Some are harmless, some are good for us and others are extremely dangerous to our health. And scientists need to study them constantly.

The technique of finding and identifying bacteria goes back into early history: bread making for example involves the controlled use of the tiny organisms we call yeast to help bread rise with their output of carbon dioxide. The production of beer too needs yeast. And some antibiotics used to treat illnesses caused by bacteria are in turn made by other micro-organisms.

To grow or 'culture' and identify bacteria, scientists need to transfer these bugs from wherever they are found to a controlled environment where they can be studied. Scientists found out long ago that the best place to grow and observe bacteria is on agar plates known as petri dishes. Agar is an extract of seaweed and has the texture and appearance of jelly.

Oxoid Ltd based in Basingstoke buys agar as a dry powder to which it adds nutrients to provide an ideal growth medium for bacteria of all kinds. Basingstoke's Wade Road is the Headquarters of the Oxoid Group with around 360 employees.

Oxoid has become the world's third largest manufacturer and distributor of microbiological culture media and other diagnostic products, with 80 per cent of sales coming from exports.

Basingstoke is the main production site, with Perth in Scotland, Wesel in Germany and Ottawa in Canada being production units converting the media from Basingstoke into a ready to use format.

Top right: The Oxo cube factory in Southwark, Oxoid's original site. Above right: Sir Humphrey Prideaux (centre), chairman of Brooke Bond pictured on a visit to Basingstoke, with Dr James Elstub (right), managing director of Oxoid, in 1976.

The origins of Oxoid go back to the 19th century when the science of bacteriology was also beginning. The original company, the Liebig Extract of Meat Company or Lemco, manufactured meat extracts which could be used in laboratories to grow bacteria. Lemco produced a popular and cheaper version of its meat extract around the turn of the century and named it Oxo - with the familiar Oxo cube first appearing just a few years later.

consumer market. Both parts of that new company continued to grow adding more subsidiaries and developing immunological products for the microbiology market.

By 1996 Unilever had decided to concentrate on consumer products resulting in a separation of Unipath from Oxoid. Following a management buy out Oxoid became an independent company at the beginning of 1997.

Continued expansion through new subsidiaries and novel products has remained the major aim and achievement of Oxoid which now looks forward to fresh challenges and triumphs in the 21st century.

Meanwhile the company fosters good relations with the local community having for example supported a local school laboratory refurbishment programme and been actively involved with the Basingstoke College of Technology and the local careers service.

No-one who has taken O level biology or has watched a modern detective series on television will have failed to have either handled, or seen, petri dishes filled with agar jelly. But how many of us in seeing that familiar product ever gave much thought to what agar jelly was, or indeed where it might be manufactured? The truth is that the world as we know it today requires many products for which we spare little thought but which in truth have an extraordinary bearing on our lives.

Top left: An aerial view of the Basingstoke site in 1975. Above left: Delegates gather in Basingstoke for an International Marketing Conference in 1976. Below: The Aura Image pc screen, the very latest testing equipment developed by Oxoid.

The Oxoid name was first used in 1924 to brand glandular extracts and other products sold to hospitals and laboratories. By the 1950s modern pharmaceuticals had replaced the earlier glandular extracts used in treating patients and the Oxoid brand became synonymous with dehydrated culture media. In 1965, rather than just being the medical division of Oxo, Oxoid Ltd was set up as a separate company.

In 1968 the Liebig company merged with Brooke Bond and in 1975 Oxoid left the Oxo cube factory in Southwark where the company was founded and moved to its present premises in Basingstoke; at the same time a number of subsidiaries were set up in Europe, Canada and Australia.

The Basingstoke site was expanded in 1980 with the building of a warehouse.

In 1984 Brooke Bond was in turn acquired by Unilever and Oxoid became part of its Medical Products Group. Oxoid was later merged with Unipath, a diagnostics company then developing pregnancy tests and similar products for the

Building a future from the past

The Manor House, The Old Rectory and The Pheasantry. What do these and many other similarly evocatively-named homes have in common? The answer is that they have all been the subject of extensive and sympathetic restoration by building contractors RW Armstrong & Sons Ltd.

One of the greatest sources of pride in Britain, and the reason many foreign tourists love the English countryside, is its architectural heritage. Visitors to these shores are frequently amazed at the vast number of architectural gems which litter the landscape with many individual villages in England containing more 17th century buildings than exist in the whole of North America.

But such a heritage will not last if it is not maintained. Indeed much of that legacy has already been lost to developers in the 1950s and 60s. Other buildings simply collapsed from neglect. Older readers will recall the dilapidated state of many village

Above centre: Roland Walter and Vera Armstrong, founders of the business. Below and right: A derelict mill which the firm refurbished in the late 1960s.

properties in the years before and after the second world war before cheap transport and the flood of commuters made such homes increasingly attractive and hence valuable.

But such value is not merely financial or personal; the nation as a whole has a vested interest in preserving the country's glories and that concern has been given solid form in the shape of availability of grants for maintenance and restoration work. Restoration, however, requires specialist skills - and fortunately one local firm has those skills in abundance.

RW Armstrong & Sons Ltd, based in Sherborne St John, is a family company spanning three generations. The firm aims to provide Architects and Interior Designers with a fully comprehensive service for substantial works to large country

homes. From the experienced management team through long serving directly employed site personnel to the apprentices that are still traditionally trained and brought up through the firm.

With a directly employed workforce of 80-90 craftsmen, the firm is one of the few to have the resources to cover all aspects of building work. Long term relationships with specialist sub-contractors add to the comprehensive list of resources.

Many of the firm's craftsmen are trained and experienced in the more specialised areas of their craft such as specialist paint techniques, running decorative plaster cornice and mouldings, the use of traditional lime putty in brickwork and plastering, as well as purpose-made joinery.

The company runs a large joinery shop in which it faithfully reproduces period woodwork such as doors, windows, stairs and mouldings as well as designing and manufacturing high-quality bedroom and kitchen furniture.

The company was established in 1957 by Mr RW Armstrong who, prior to branching out on his own, had been foreman for a larger local building company, HN Edwards & Partners.

RW Armstrong set himself up building small extensions on local village houses. Initially he ran the business from his home in Sherborne St John helped by his wife Vera and was joined some years later by their two sons Brian and Colin. Since then a third generation has joined the firm.

Today this family building company is actively involved in various restoration and new build projects within a fifty mile radius of its base in Aldermaston Road, Sherbourne St John. Almost all of the company's work is in the form of alterations, extensions and refurbishment of various country houses and listed buildings including churches, barns, cottages and manor houses - and always to a very high specification. From its humble beginnings today's clients include Earls, Lords, and Knights, prestigious corporations such as Barclays Bank and the BBC, as well as countless less prominent, though no less important, names. Projects have ranged from modest alterations to contracts of more than £4m in value, such as the renovation of a small country estate at Brown Candover, near Basingstoke.

The firm is on the list of approved contractors for English Heritage, SPAB, the National Trust and Local Authority conservation departments.

'Gee, will you look at that!' is the well known cry of the American tourist passing through the leafy lanes of England; there are few things to delight the eye more than the sight of a classic English building restored to the highest of standards. RW Armstrong & Sons Ltd is helping ensure that that our heritage of architectural beauty will remain with us for many more centuries to come.

Top left: A charming thatched cottage recently built from new. Top right: One of the many indoor pools constructed by the company. Right: The current directors, Nigel, Brian and Colin Armstrong.

A snowy market day during the winter of 1962 when only a few brave stallholders and a few even braver shoppers tackled the elements

Acknowledgments

Editorial captions were compiled by Ernie Major BA, from photographs provided by the Willis Museum and Robert Brown.

Much of the material was provided by Robert Brown and as a result of interviews conducted by Basingstoke Talking History, a project run by the Basingstoke Archaeological & Historical Society with the Willis Museum.

Research was carried out by Barbara Applin, Kate Mattock, Diane Grudgings, Arthur Attwood and Rebecca Saxton.

Our thanks are also due to Steve Ainsworth for his copywriting skills.